METHOD AND MADNESS

METHOD AND MADNESS

The hidden story
of Israel's assaults on Gaza

NORMAN G. FINKELSTEIN

OR Books
New York · London

© 2014 Norman G. Finkelstein

Published by OR Books, New York and London
Visit our website at **www.orbooks.com**

First printing 2014

Cataloging-in-Publication data is available from the Library of
    Congress.
A catalog record for this book is available from the British Library.

ISBN 978-1-939293-71-8 paperback
ISBN 978-1-939293-72-5 e-book

Cover design by Bathcat Ltd.
Cover photograph: Israel's bombing of Gaza with white phosphorus
during Operation Cast Lead, January 2009 (Human Rights Watch).

This book is set in Amalia. Typeset by CBIGS Group, Chennai, India.
Printed by BookMobile in the US and CPI Books Ltd in the UK.

To

Rudy, Carolyn, and Allan

This is a battle for hearts and minds. The IDF will make every effort to clearly demonstrate it can fight terrorism and win, thereby cementing itself in the enemy's psyche as a beast one should not provoke.

—Veteran Israeli journalist Ron Ben-Yishai
on Operation Protective Edge

TABLE OF CONTENTS

PREFACE

Israel has committed three massacres in Gaza during the past five years: Operation Cast Lead (2008–9), Operation Pillar of Defense (2012), and Operation Protective Edge (2014). It also killed in 2010 nine foreign nationals aboard a humanitarian vessel (the *Mavi Marmara*) en route to deliver basic goods to Gaza's besieged population.

This book chronicles and analyzes these various Israeli assaults. It casts doubt on the accepted interpretation of their key triggers, features, and consequences. Each chapter reproduces (with minor stylistic changes) the author's commentary as it was composed after each successive assault. The year in each chapter heading indicates when it was written.

A trio of themes form the connective tissue of the book's narrative. First, Israel has repeatedly manufactured pretexts to achieve larger political objectives.

Invariably, it resorted to military action against Hamas in order to provoke a violent response. Israel then exploited Hamas's retaliation to launch a series of murderous assaults on Gaza.

Second, Israel has time and again eluded accountability for its war crimes and crimes against humanity. Both the Goldstone Report and Turkey's attempt to prosecute Israel after the *Mavi Marmara* massacre proved stillborn. An International Criminal Court indictment of Israeli leaders after Operation Protective Edge also seems unlikely.

Third, at the end of each new round, the political balance between the antagonists did not change: each side declared victory, but neither side won. Such a stalemate has been much more tolerable for Israel than for the people of Gaza. The human and material losses suffered by Gazans have been of an incomparably greater magnitude. Moreover, Israel can live with the status quo, whereas Gaza, suffering under the double yoke of a foreign occupation and an illegal blockade, cannot. The fact that the indomitable will of the people of Gaza has repeatedly brought the Israeli killing machine to a standstill cannot but impress. However, such "negative" victories have yet to translate into a "positive" victory of a real improvement in Gaza's daily life.

Palestinians are under neither legal nor moral obligation to desist from using armed force against Israel. Nonetheless, it is this author's contention that nonviolent mass resistance, both in Gaza *and by its supporters abroad*, still offers the best prospect for ending the illegal siege and occupation. Armed resistance has been attempted many times and, notwithstanding its heroism and nobility, has failed to budge Israel a jot. The time is ripe to attempt militant nonviolent resistance, or so it is argued in the ensuing pages.

Norman G. Finkelstein
September 2014

ACKNOWLEDGMENTS

I am grateful to Maren Hackmann-Mahajan and Jamie Stern-Weiner for both their editorial skills and the pleasures of collaborating with them. I am also indebted to the many individuals who forwarded me important information and read earlier drafts of this manuscript.

1/ PEACE OFFENSIVE (2011)

"IF ONLY IT WOULD JUST SINK INTO THE SEA," Prime Minister Yitzhak Rabin despaired just before signing the 1993 Oslo Accord.[1] Although Israel had always coveted Gaza, its stubborn resistance eventually caused the occupier to sour on the Strip. In April 2004, Prime Minister Ariel Sharon announced that Israel would "disengage" from Gaza, and by September 2005 both Israeli troops and Jewish settlers had been pulled out. It would relieve international pressure on Israel and consequently "freez[e] ... the political process," a close advisor to Sharon explained, laying out the rationale behind the disengagement. "And when you freeze that process you prevent the establishment of a Palestinian state." Harvard political economist Sara Roy observed that "with the disengagement from Gaza, the Sharon government was clearly seeking to preclude any return to political negotiations ... while preserving and deepening its hold on Palestine."[2] Israel subsequently declared that it was no longer the occupying power in Gaza. However, human rights organizations and international institutions rejected this contention because, in myriad ways, Israel still preserved near-total dominance of the Strip. "Whether the Israeli army is inside Gaza or redeployed around its periphery," Human Rights Watch (HRW) concluded, "it remains in control."[3] Indeed, Israel's own leading authority on international law, Yoram Dinstein, aligned himself with the "prevalent opinion" that the Israeli occupation of Gaza was not over.[4]

In January 2006, disgusted by years of official corruption and fruitless negotiations, Palestinians elected the Islamic movement Hamas into office. Israel immediately tightened its blockade of Gaza, and the US joined in. It was demanded of the newly elected government that it renounce violence, and recognize Israel as well as prior Israeli-Palestinian agreements. These preconditions for international engagement were unilateral, not reciprocal. Israel wasn't required to renounce violence. It wasn't compelled to withdraw from the occupied territories, enabling Palestinians to exercise *their* right to statehood. And, whereas Hamas was obliged to recognize prior agreements, such as the Oslo Accord, which undercut basic Palestinian rights,[5] Israel was free to eviscerate prior agreements, such as the 2003 "Road Map."[6]

In June 2007, Hamas consolidated its control over Gaza when it preempted a coup attempt orchestrated by Washington in league with Israel and elements of the Palestinian Authority (PA).[7] After Hamas checked this "democracy promotion" initiative of US President George W. Bush, Israel and Washington retaliated by tightening the screws on Gaza yet further. In June 2008, Hamas and Israel entered into a cease-fire brokered by Egypt, but in November of that year Israel violated the cease-fire by carrying out a bloody border raid on Gaza. Israel's modus operandi recalled a February 1955 border raid during the buildup to the 1956 Sinai invasion.[8] The objective, then and now, was to instigate a backlash that Israel could exploit as a pretext for a full-blown assault.

On 27 December 2008, Israel launched Operation Cast Lead.[9] The first week consisted of air attacks, followed on 3 January 2009 by a combined air and ground assault. Piloting the most advanced combat aircraft in the world, the Israeli air corps flew nearly 3,000 sorties over Gaza and dropped 1,000 tons of explosives, while the Israeli army deployment comprised several brigades equipped with sophisticated intelligence-gathering systems and weaponry, such as robotic and TV-aided remote-controlled guns. During the attack, Palestinian armed groups fired some 925 mostly rudimentary "rockets" (and an additional number of mortar shells) into Israel. On 18 January, a cease-fire went into effect, but the economic strangulation of Gaza continued.

Israel officially justified Cast Lead on the grounds of self-defense against Hamas "rocket" attacks.[10] Such a rationale did not, however, withstand even superficial scrutiny. If Israel had wanted to avert the Hamas rocket attacks, it would not have triggered them by breaking the June 2008 cease-fire with Hamas. Israel also could have opted for renewing—and then honoring—the cease-fire. In fact, as a former Israeli intelligence officer told the Crisis Group, "the cease-fire options on the table after the war were in place there before it."[11] More broadly, Israel could have reached a diplomatic settlement with the Palestinian leadership that resolved the conflict and terminated armed hostilities. Insofar as the declared objective of Cast Lead was to destroy the "infrastructure of terrorism," Israel's alibi of self-defense appeared even less credible after the invasion: over-whelmingly the Israel Defense Forces (IDF) targeted not Hamas strongholds but "decidedly 'non-terrorist,' non-Hamas" sites.[12]

A close look at Israeli actions sustains the conclusion that the massive death and destruction visited on Gaza were not an accidental byproduct of the 2008–9 invasion but its barely concealed objective. To deflect culpability for this premeditated slaughter, Israel persistently alleged that Palestinian casualties resulted from Hamas's use of civilians as "human shields." Indeed, throughout its attack, Israel strove to manipulate perceptions by controlling press reports and otherwise tilting Western coverage in its favor. But the allegation that Hamas used civilians as human shields was not borne out by human rights investigations, while the gap between Israel's claim that it did everything possible to avoid "collateral damage" and the hundreds of bodies of women and children dug out of the rubble was too vast to bridge.

"The attacks that caused the greatest number of fatalities and injuries," Amnesty International found in its post-invasion inquiry, were carried out with long-range high-precision munitions fired from combat aircraft, helicopters and drones, or from tanks stationed up to several kilometers away—often against preselected targets, a process that would normally require approval from up the chain of command. The victims of these attacks were not caught in the crossfire of battles between Palestinian militants and Israeli forces, nor were they shielding militants or other legitimate targets. Many were killed when their homes were bombed while they slept. Others were going about their daily activities in their homes, sitting in their yard, hanging the laundry on the roof when they were targeted in air strikes or tank shelling. Children were studying or playing in their bedrooms or on the roof, or outside their homes, when they were struck by missiles or tank shells.[13]

It further found that Palestinian civilians, "including women and children, were shot at short range when posing no threat to the lives of the Israeli soldiers," and that "there was no fighting going on in their vicinity when they were shot."[14] An HRW study documented Israel's killing of Palestinian civilians who "were trying to convey their noncombatant status by waving a white flag," and where "all available evidence indicates that Israeli forces had control of the areas in question, no fighting was taking place there at the time, and Palestinian fighters were not hiding among the civilians who were shot." In one instance, "two women and three children from the Abd Rabbo family were standing for a few minutes outside their home—at least three of them holding pieces of white cloth—when an Israeli soldier opened fire, killing two girls, aged two and seven, and wounding the grandmother and third girl."[15] Unabashed and undeterred, Israel still sang paeans to the IDF's unique respect for the "supreme value of human life." Israeli philosopher Asa Kasher praised the "impeccable" values of the IDF, such as "protecting the human dignity of every human being, even the most vile terrorist" and the "uniquely Israeli value . . . of the sanctity of human life."[16]

The charges and countercharges over the use of human shields were symptomatic of Israel's attempt to obfuscate what actually happened on the ground. In fact,

Israel began its public relations preparations six months before Cast Lead, and a centralized body in the prime minister's office, the National Information Directorate, was specifically tasked with coordinating Israeli *hasbara* (propaganda).[17] Nonetheless, after world opinion turned against Israel, influential military analyst Anthony Cordesman opined that, if it was now isolated, it was because Israel had not sufficiently invested in the "war of perceptions": Israel "did little to explain the steps it was taking to minimize civilian casualties and collateral damage on the world stage"; it "certainly could—and should—have done far more to show its level of military restraint and make it credible."[18] Israelis "are execrable at public relations," Haaretz.com senior editor Bradley Burston weighed in, while according to respected Israeli political scientist Shlomo Avineri the world took a dim view of the Gaza invasion because of "the name given to the operation, which greatly affects the way in which it will be perceived."[19] But if the micromanaged PR blitz ultimately did not convince, the problem was not that Israel failed to convey adequately its humanitarian mission or that the whole world misperceived what happened. Rather, it was that the scope of the massacre was so appalling that no amount of propaganda could disguise it.

What explains Israel's brutal assault on a civilian population? Early speculation centered on the upcoming Israeli elections, scheduled to be held in February 2009. Jockeying for votes was no doubt a factor in this Sparta-like society consumed by "revenge and the thirst for blood."[20] However, the principal motives for the Gaza invasion were to be found not in the election cycle but, first, in the need to restore Israel's "deterrence capacity," and, second, in the need to counter the threat posed by a new Palestinian "peace offensive."

Israel's "larger concern" in Operation Cast Lead, *New York Times* Middle East correspondent Ethan Bronner reported, quoting Israeli sources, was to "re-establish Israeli deterrence," because "its enemies are less afraid of it than they once were, or should be."[21] Preserving its "deterrence capacity" has always loomed large in Israeli strategic doctrine. In fact, it was a primary impetus behind Israel's first strike against Egypt in June 1967 that resulted in Israel's occupation of Gaza and the West Bank. To justify Cast Lead, Israeli historian Benny Morris wrote that "many Israelis feel that the walls ... are closing in ... much as they felt in early June 1967."[22] Ordinary Israelis were no doubt filled with foreboding in June 1967, but Israel did not face an existential threat at the time (as Morris knows[23]) and Israeli leaders were not apprehensive about the war's outcome. Multiple US intelligence agencies had concluded that the Egyptians did not intend to attack Israel and that, in the improbable case that they did, alone or in concert with other Arab countries, Israel would—in President Lyndon Johnson's words—"whip the hell out of them."[24] The head of the Mossad told senior American officials just before Israel attacked that "there were no differences between the US and the Israelis on the military intelligence picture or its interpretation."[25]

The predicament for Israel lay elsewhere. Spurred by Egyptian President Gamal Abdel Nasser's "radical" nationalism, which climaxed in his defiant gestures in May 1967,[26] the Arab world had come to imagine that it could defy Israeli orders with impunity. Israel was losing its "deterrence capability," Divisional Commander Ariel

Sharon admonished Israeli cabinet members hesitant to launch a first strike, "our main weapon—*the fear of us*."[27] In effect, "deterrence capacity" denoted, not warding off an imminent lethal blow, but instead keeping Arabs so intimidated that they could not even conceive challenging Israel's freedom to carry on as it pleased, however ruthlessly and recklessly. Israel unleashed the war on 5 June 1967, according to Israeli strategic analyst Zeev Maoz, "to restore the credibility of Israeli deterrence."[28]

At the start of the new millennium, Israel confronted another challenge to its deterrence capacity. After a nearly two-decade-long guerrilla war, Hezbollah had ejected the Israeli occupying army from Lebanon in May 2000. The fact that Israel suffered a mortifying defeat, one celebrated throughout the Arab world, made another war well-nigh inevitable. Israel almost immediately began planning for the next round,[29] and in summer 2006 found a pretext when Hezbollah captured two Israeli soldiers inside Israel (several others were killed during the operation) and in exchange for their release demanded the freedom of Lebanese prisoners held by Israel. Although Israel unleashed the full fury of its air force and geared up for a ground invasion, it suffered yet another ignominious defeat. One indication of Israel's reversal of fortune was that, unlike in any of its previous armed conflicts, in the final stages of the 2006 war it fought not in defiance of a UN cease-fire resolution but in the hope that a UN resolution would rescue it from an unwinnable situation. "Frustration with the conduct and outcome of the Second Lebanon War," an influential Israeli think tank reported, prompted Israel to "initiate a thorough internal examination . . . on the order of 63 different commissions of inquiry."[30]

After the 2006 Lebanon War, Israel was itching to take on Hezbollah again but was not yet confident it would emerge triumphant from the battle. In mid-2008, Israel sought to conscript the US for an attack on Iran, which it believed would also decapitate Hezbollah (Iran's junior partner), and thereby humble key rivals to its regional hegemony. To Israel's chagrin and humiliation, Washington vetoed an attack and Iran went its merry way; the credibility of Israel's capacity to terrorize slipped another notch. It was time to find another target, and Gaza fit the bill. It was largely defenseless while Hamas had resisted Israeli diktat, crowing first, in 2005, that it had forced Israel to "withdraw" and then, in 2008, that it had forced Israel to accept a cease-fire. If Gaza was *where*

Israel would restore its deterrence capacity, one theater of the 2006 Lebanon war had already hinted at *how* it might successfully be done.

During the 2006 Lebanon war, Israel pulverized the southern suburb of Beirut known as the Dahiya, which was home to many poor Shiite supporters of Hezbollah. In the war's aftermath Israeli military officers began referring to the "Dahiya strategy." "We will wield disproportionate power against every village from which shots are fired on Israel, and cause immense damage and destruction," IDF Northern Command Chief Gadi Eisenkot anticipated. "This isn't a suggestion. This is a plan that has already been authorized." In the event of future hostilities, Israel needed "to act immediately, decisively, and with force that is disproportionate," reserve Colonel Gabriel Siboni of the Israeli Institute for National Security Studies declared. "Such a response aims at inflicting damage and meting out punishment to an extent that will demand long and expensive reconstruction processes." "The next war . . . will lead to the elimination of the Lebanese military, the destruction of the national infrastructure, and intense suffering among the population," former chief of the Israeli National Security

Council Giora Eiland threatened. "Serious damage to the Republic of Lebanon, the destruction of homes and infrastructure, and the suffering of hundreds of thousands of people are consequences that can influence Hezbollah's behavior more than anything else."[31]

Under international law, use of disproportionate force and targeting of civilian infrastructure constitute war crimes. Besides Lebanon, Gaza was frequently singled out as a prime target of Israel's criminal strategy. "Too bad it did not take hold immediately after the [2005] 'disengagement' from Gaza and the first rocket barrages," a respected Israeli pundit lamented. "Had we immediately adopted the Dahiya strategy, we would have likely spared ourselves much trouble." If and when Palestinians launched another rocket attack, Israeli Interior Minister Meir Sheetrit urged in late September 2008, "the IDF should . . . decide on a neighborhood in Gaza and level it."[32]

The operative Israeli plan for Cast Lead could be gleaned from authoritative statements issued after it got underway: "What we have to do is act systematically with the aim of punishing all the organizations that are firing the rockets and mortars, as well as the civilians who are enabling them to fire and hide" (reserve Major-General Amiram Levin); "After this operation there will not be one Hamas building left standing in Gaza" (Deputy IDF Chief of Staff Dan Harel); "Anything affiliated with Hamas is a legitimate target" (IDF Spokesperson Major Avital Leibowitz); "It [should be] possible to destroy Gaza, so they will understand not to mess with us. . . . It is a great opportunity to demolish thousands of houses of all the terrorists, so they will think twice before they launch rockets. . . . I hope the operation will come to an end with great achievements and with the complete destruction of terrorism and Hamas. In my opinion, they should be razed to the ground, so thousands of houses, tunnels and industries will be demolished" (Deputy Prime Minister Eli Yishai). The military correspondent for Israel Channel 10 News commented, "Israel isn't trying to hide the fact that it reacts disproportionately."[33]

Israeli media exulted at the "shock and awe" (*Maariv*) of its opening air campaign, which was designed to "engender a sense of dread."[34] Whereas Israel killed a mere 55 Lebanese during the first two days of the 2006 war, it killed as many as 300 Gazans in four minutes on the first day of Cast Lead. Most targets were located in "densely populated residential areas," while the bombardments began "at around 11:30 a.m., a busy time, when the streets were full of civilians, including school children leaving classes at the end of the morning shift and those going to school for the second shift."[35] Several days into the slaughter an Israeli strategic analyst observed, "The IDF, which planned to attack buildings and sites populated by hundreds of people, did not warn them in advance to leave, but intended to kill a great many of them, and succeeded."[36] Benny Morris lauded "Israel's highly efficient air assault on Hamas," and an American military analyst marveled at the "masterful precision" of the assault.[37] The Israeli columnist B. Michael was less impressed by the dispatch of helicopter gunships and jet planes "over a giant prison and firing at its people."[38] For example, on that first day of Cast Lead, Israeli aerial strikes killed or fatally injured at least 16 children while an Israeli drone-launched precision missile killed nine college students (two of them young women) "who were waiting for a UN bus" to take them home.[39]

As Cast Lead proceeded apace, prominent Israelis dropped all pretenses that its purpose was to stop Hamas rocket fire. "Remember, [Israeli Defense Minister Ehud]

Barak's real foe is not Hamas," a former Israeli minister told the Crisis Group. "It is the memory of 2006."[40] Israeli pundits gloated that "Gaza is to Lebanon as the second sitting for an exam is to the first—a second chance to get it right," and that, this time around, Israel had "hurled [Gaza] back," not 20 years as it promised to do in Lebanon, but "into the 1940s. Electricity is available only for a few hours a day"; that "Israel regained its deterrence capabilities" because "the war in Gaza has compensated for the shortcomings of the [2006] Second Lebanon War"; and that "there is no doubt that Hezbollah leader Hassan Nasrallah is upset these days. . . . There will no longer be anyone in the Arab world who can claim that Israel is weak."[41]

New York Times foreign affairs expert Thomas Friedman joined in the chorus of hallelujahs. Israel actually won the 2006 war, Friedman reasoned, because it had inflicted "substantial property damage and collateral casualties on Lebanon," and consequently administered an "education" to Hezbollah: fearing the Lebanese people's wrath, Hezbollah would "think three times next time" before defying Israel. He expressed hope that Israel would also "'educate' Hamas by inflicting a heavy death toll on Hamas militants and heavy pain on the Gaza population."[42]

If Israel targeted the Lebanese civilian population and infrastructure during the 2006 war, it was not because it had no choice, but because terrorizing Lebanese civilians appeared to be a low-cost method of "education." This pedagogical approach was much preferred to tangling with a determined foe, such as the Party of God, and suffering heavy combatant casualties. Whereas Hezbollah's unexpectedly fierce resistance prevented Israel from claiming a victory on the battlefield, Israel did successfully educate the civilian Lebanese population, which is why Hezbollah was careful not to antagonize Israel during Cast Lead.[43] Israel's pedagogy also proved a success among the Gaza population. "It was hard to convince Gazans whose homes were demolished and family and friends killed and injured," the Crisis Group reported, "that this amounted to 'victory,'" as Hamas had boasted in the wake of the invasion.[44] In the case of Gaza, Israel could also lay claim to a military victory, but only because—in the words of Israeli journalist Gideon Levy—"a large, broad army is fighting against a helpless population and a weak, ragged organization that has fled the conflict zones and is barely putting up a fight."[45]

Israel's evolving modus operandi for restoring its deterrence capacity describes a curve steadily regressing into barbarism. Israel gained its victory in 1967 primarily on the battlefield—albeit in a "turkey shoot"[46]—while in subsequent hostilities, mostly in Lebanon, it sought both to achieve a battlefield victory and to bombard the civilian population into submission. But Israel targeted Gaza to restore its deterrence capacity because it eschewed *any* of the risks of a conventional war; it targeted Gaza *because* it was largely defenseless. Israel's resort to unalloyed terror in turn revealed its relative decline as a military power, while the glorification of its military prowess during and after Cast Lead by the likes of Benny Morris registered the growing detachment of Israeli intellectuals, and a good share of the public as well, from reality.

A supplementary benefit of this deterrence strategy was that it restored Israel's domestic morale. A 2009 internal UN document concluded that the invasion's "one significant achievement" was that it dispelled doubts among Israelis about "their ability and the power of the IDF to issue a blow to its enemies. . . . The use of 'excessive force' ... proves Israel is the landlord.... The pictures of destruction were intended more for Israeli eyes than those of Israel's enemies, eyes starved of revenge and national pride."[47]

Beyond restoring its deterrence capacity, Israel's principal goal in the Gaza invasion was to fend off the latest threat posed by Palestinian pragmatism. Except for Israel backed by the United States, the international community has consistently supported a settlement of the Israel-Palestine conflict that calls for two states based on a full Israeli withdrawal to its prewar 1967 borders, and a "just" resolution of the refugee question based on the right of return and compensation.[48] The lop-sided voting record on the annual UN General Assembly resolution "Peaceful Settlement of the Question of Palestine" as well as the 2004 advisory opinion of the International Court of Justice attest to this broad consensus. It is further evidenced by an Arab League peace initiative of 2002 (later reaffirmed) that commits League members to not just recognizing Israel but also establishing "normal relations" once Israel implements the consensus terms for a comprehensive peace. The Arab Peace Initiative was subsequently adopted by all 57 members of the Organization of the Islamic Conference, including Iran.[49]

It is acknowledged on all sides that the Palestinian Authority has accepted the terms of the global consensus and even expressed willingness to make significant concessions going beyond it.[50] But what about Hamas, which currently governs Gaza? A recent study by a US government agency concluded that Hamas "has been carefully and consciously adjusting its political program for years and has sent repeated signals that it is ready to begin a process of coexisting with Israel."[51] Khalid Mishal, the head of Hamas's politburo, stated in a March 2008 interview, for example, that "most Palestinian forces, including Hamas, accept a state on the 1967 borders."[52] Even right after the devastation wrought by Cast Lead, Mishal reiterated that "the objective remains the constitution of a Palestinian state with East Jerusalem as its capital, the return of the Israelis to the pre-67 borders and the right of return of our refugees."[53] In a complementary formulation, Mishal told former US president Jimmy Carter in 2006 (and later reaffirmed in a Damascus press conference) that "Hamas agreed to accept any peace agreement negotiated between the leaders of the PLO [Palestine Liberation Organization] and Israel provided it is subsequently approved by Palestinians in a referendum or by a democratically elected government."[54]

From the mid-1990s onward, Hamas "rarely, if at all" adverted to its notoriously anti-Semitic charter and now "no longer cites or refers" to it.[55] Israeli officials knew full well before Cast Lead that, the charter notwithstanding, a diplomatic settlement could have been reached with Hamas. "The Hamas leadership has recognized that its ideological goal is not attainable and will not be in the foreseeable future," former Mossad head Ephraim Levy observed. "They are ready and willing to see the establishment of a Palestinian state in the temporary borders of 1967. . . . They know that the moment a Palestinian state is established with their cooperation, they will be obligated to change the rules of the game: They will have to adopt a path that could lead them far from their original ideological goals."[56]

After having rejected Hamas's cease-fire proposals for months, Israel finally agreed to them in June 2008.[57] Hamas was "careful to maintain the cease-fire," a semi-official Israeli publication reported, despite Israel's reneging on the crucial quid pro quo that it substantially lift the economic blockade of Gaza. "The lull was sporadically violated by rocket and mortar shell fire, carried out by rogue terrorist organizations," the Israeli source continued. "At the same time, the [Hamas] movement tried to enforce the terms of the arrangement on the other terrorist organizations and to prevent them from violating it."[58] The Islamic movement had on this occasion stood by its word, making it a credible negotiating partner. And unlike the hapless PA, which was doing Israel's bidding but getting no returns, Hamas appeared to extract concessions from Israel. As a result, Hamas's stock among Palestinians increased.

Hamas's acquiescence in the two-state settlement and its honoring of the cease-fire agreement proved a daunting challenge to Israel. It could no longer justify shunning Hamas; it would be only a matter of time before the Europeans renewed dialogue and relations with the organization. The prospect of an incoming US administration negotiating with Iran and Hamas, and edging closer to the international consensus for settling the Israel-Palestine conflict, which some policymakers in Washington now advocated,[59] threatened to further spotlight Israel's intransigence and isolate it diplomatically.

Israel needed to provoke Hamas into taking up arms again. Once hostilities broke out, Israel could radicalize or destroy Hamas, eliminating it as a legitimate negotiating partner or as an obstacle to a final agreement on Israel's terms.

It was not the first time Israel had confronted such a threat—an Arab peace initiative, tentative Palestinian support for a two-state settlement, and a Palestinian cease-fire— and not the first time it had embarked on provocation and war to nip it in the bud. "By the late 1970s," a pair of Israeli scholars recalled, "the two-state solution had won the support of the Palestinian leadership in the occupied territories as well as that of most Arab states and other members of the international community."[60] In addition, PLO leaders headquartered in Lebanon strictly adhered to a cease-fire with Israel negotiated in July 1981.[61] In August 1981, Saudi Arabia unveiled a peace plan (later approved by the Arab League) based on the two-state settlement.[62]

Reacting to these dire developments, Israel stepped up preparations to destroy the PLO.[63] In his analysis of the buildup to the 1982 Lebanon war, an Israeli strategic analyst reported that PLO leader Yasser Arafat was contemplating a historic compromise with the "Zionist state," whereas "all Israeli cabinets since 1967" as well as "leading mainstream doves" opposed a Palestinian state. Fearing diplomatic pressures, Israel maneuvered to sabotage the two-state settlement by eliminating the PLO as a potential negotiating partner. It conducted punitive military raids "deliberately out of proportion" against "Palestinian and Lebanese civilians" in order to weaken "PLO moderates," strengthen the hand of Arafat's "radical rivals," and guarantee the PLO's "inflexibility."

Still, Israel eventually had to choose between a pair of stark options: "a political move leading to a historic compromise with the PLO, or preemptive military action against it." To fend off Arafat's "peace offensive"— the Israeli analyst's telling phrase—Israel embarked on military action in June 1982. The Israeli invasion "had been preceded by more than a year of effective cease-fire with the PLO." But after murderous Israeli provocations, the last of which left as many as 200 civilians dead (including 60 occupants of a Palestinian children's hospital), the PLO finally retaliated, causing a single Israeli casualty. Although Israel exploited the PLO's resumption of attacks on northern Israel as a pretext for its invasion (Operation Peace for Galilee), the Israeli analyst

concluded that the "raison d'être of the entire operation" was "destroying the PLO as a political force capable
of claiming a Palestinian state on the West Bank."[64]

Fast forward to the eve of Cast Lead in December
2008. Israeli Foreign Minister Tzipi Livni stated that
whereas Israel wanted to create a temporary period of
calm with Hamas, an extended truce "harms the Israeli
strategic goal, empowers Hamas, and gives the impression that Israel recognizes the movement."[65] Transla-
tion: a protracted cease-fire, which cast a bright light on
Hamas's pragmatism in word and deed and consequently
increased international pressure on Israel to negotiate a
diplomatic settlement, would undermine Israel's strategic goal of retaining the West Bank. Israel had already
resolved to attack Hamas as far back as March 2007 and
only acquiesced in the June 2008 truce because "the
Israeli army needed time to prepare."[66]

Once all the pieces were in place, Israel still required
a pretext to abort the cease-fire. A careful study covering
the period 2000–2008 demonstrated that "overwhelmingly" it was "Israel that kills first after conflict pauses."[67]
After the Gaza redeployment in late 2005, it was Israel
that broke the de facto truce with Hamas that began in

April 2005 and, after Hamas won the 2006 elections, it was Israel that persisted in its illegal practice of "targeted assassinations" despite a Hamas cease-fire.[68] Again on 4 November 2008, while the American public and media were riveted to the election-day returns that elevated Barack Obama to the presidency, Israel broke the cease-fire. On the spurious pretext of preempting a Hamas raid, it killed Palestinian militants, knowing full well that it would provoke Hamas into hitting back.[69] "A cease-fire agreed in June between Israel and Palestinian armed groups in Gaza held for four-and-a-half months," Amnesty observed in its annual report, "but broke down after Israeli forces killed six Palestinian militants in air strikes and other attacks on 4 November."[70]

The predictable sequel to Israel's attack was that Hamas resumed its rocket attacks—"in retaliation," as the Israeli Intelligence and Terrorism Information Center wrote.[71] Still, Hamas was "interested in renewing the relative calm with Israel," according to Israeli internal security chief Yuval Diskin, and Hamas would have accepted a "bargain" in which it "would halt the fire in exchange for easing of . . . Israeli policies [that] have kept a choke hold on the economy of the Strip," according to former IDF commander in Gaza Shmuel Zakai.[72] But Israel tightened yet again the illegal economic blockade of Gaza while demanding a unilateral and unconditional cease-fire by Hamas. Even before Israel intensified the blockade, former UN High Commissioner for Human Rights Mary Robinson decried its effects: Gaza's "whole civilization has been destroyed, I'm not exaggerating."[73] By December 2008, Israel had brought Gaza's infrastructure "to the brink of collapse," according to an Israeli human rights organization.[74] "Food, medicine, fuel, parts for water and sanitation systems, fertilizer, plastic sheeting, phones, paper, glue, shoes and even teacups are no longer getting through in sufficient quantities or at all," Sara Roy reported. "The breakdown of an entire society is happening in front of us, but there is little international response beyond UN warnings which are ignored."[75]

If Hamas had stayed passive after the 4 November killings, Israel would almost certainly have ratcheted up its provocations, just as it did in the lead-up to the 1982 war, until restraint became politically untenable for the Islamic movement. In any event, faced with the prospect of an asphyxiating Israeli blockade even if it ceased firing rockets, and thus forced to choose between "starvation and fighting,"[76] Hamas opted for resistance, albeit largely symbolic. "You cannot just land blows, leave the Palestinians in Gaza in the economic distress they're in, and expect that Hamas will just sit around and do nothing," the former IDF commander in Gaza observed.[77] "Our modest, home-made rockets," Khalid Mishal wrote in an open letter during Cast Lead, "are our cry of protest to the world."[78] But Israel could now enter a plea of self-defense to its willfully gullible Western patrons as it embarked on yet another murderous invasion. Apart from minor adaptations in the script—the bogey was not "PLO terrorism" but "Hamas terrorism," the pretext was not shelling in the north but rocket fire in the south—the 2008 reprise stayed remarkably faithful to the 1982 original. It derailed a functioning cease-fire and foiled another Palestinian peace offensive.[79] Israel could now breathe a deep sigh of relief.

2/ PUNISH, HUMILIATE AND TERRORIZE (2011)

IN APRIL 2009, THE PRESIDENT of the United Nations Human Rights Council (UNHRC) appointed a "Fact-Finding Mission" to "investigate all violations of international human rights law and international humanitarian law that might have been committed at any time in the context of the military operations that were conducted in Gaza during the period from 27 December 2008 and 18 January 2009, whether before, during or after."[1] Richard Goldstone, former judge of the Constitutional Court of South Africa and former Prosecutor of the International Criminal Tribunals for the former Yugoslavia and Rwanda, was named head of the Mission. The Mission's original mandate was to scrutinize only Israeli violations of human rights during Operation Cast Lead, but Goldstone made his acceptance of the job conditional on broadening the mandate to include violations by all parties. The council president invited Goldstone to write the mandate himself, which Goldstone did and which the president then accepted. "It was very difficult to refuse . . . a mandate that I'd written for myself," Goldstone later observed. Nonetheless, Israel did not cooperate with the Mission on the grounds of its alleged bias.[2] In September 2009, the long-awaited report of the Goldstone Mission was released.[3] It was a searing indictment, not just of the Gaza invasion, but also of the ongoing Israeli occupation.

The Goldstone Report found that much of the death and destruction Israel inflicted on Gaza's civilian population and infrastructure was premeditated. The assault was said to be anchored in a military doctrine that "views disproportionate destruction and creating maximum disruption in the lives of many people as a legitimate means to achieve military and political goals," and was "designed to have inevitably dire consequences for the noncombatants in Gaza."[4] The "disproportionate destruction and violence against civilians" were part of a "deliberate policy," as were the "humiliation and dehumanization of the Palestinian population."[5] Although Israel justified its assault on grounds of self-defense against Hamas rocket attacks, the Goldstone Report pointed to a different motive. The "primary purpose" of the economic blockade Israel imposed on Gaza was to "bring about a situation in which the civilian population would find life so intolerable that they would leave (if that were possible) or turn Hamas out of office, as well as to collectively punish the civilian population." The invasion itself aimed to "punish the Gaza population for its resilience and for its apparent support for Hamas, and possibly with the intent of forcing a change in such support."[6] The Report concluded that the Israeli assault on Gaza constituted "a deliberately disproportionate attack designed to punish, humiliate and terrorize a civilian population, radically diminish its local economic capacity both to work and to provide for itself, and to force upon it an ever increasing sense of dependency and vulnerability."[7] The Report also paid tribute to "the resilience and dignity" of the Gazan people "in the face of dire circumstances."[8]

The Goldstone Report found that, in seeking to "punish, humiliate and terrorize" the Gazan civilian population, Israel committed numerous violations of customary and conventional international law. It also ticked off a lengthy list of war crimes that Israel committed, such as "willful killing, torture or inhuman treatment," "willfully causing great suffering or serious injury to body or health," "extensive destruction of property, not justified by military necessity and carried out unlawfully and wantonly," and "use of human shields."[9] It further found that Israeli actions that "deprive Palestinians in the Gaza Strip of their means of sustenance, employment, housing and water, that deny their freedom of movement and their right to leave and enter their own country, that limit their access to courts of law and effective remedies . . . might justify a competent court finding that crimes against humanity have been committed."[10]

The Goldstone Report pinned primary culpability for these criminal offenses on Israel's political and military elites: "The systematic and deliberate nature of the activities . . . leave the Mission in no doubt that responsibility lies in the first place with those who designed, planned, ordered and oversaw the operations."[11] It also found that the fatalities, property damage, and "psychological trauma" resulting from Hamas's "indiscriminate" and "deliberate" rocket attacks on Israel's civilian population constituted "war crimes and may amount to crimes against humanity."[12] Because the Goldstone Mission (like human rights organizations) devoted a much smaller fraction of its findings to Hamas rocket attacks, critics accused it of bias. The accusation was valid, but its weight ran in the opposite direction. If one considers that the ratio of Palestinian to Israeli deaths stood at more than 100:1 and of dwellings ravaged at more than 6,000:1, then the proportion of the Goldstone Report given over to death and destruction caused by Hamas in Israel was *much greater* than the objective data would have warranted.[13]

When it was subsequently put to Goldstone that the Report disproportionately focused on Israeli violations of international law, he replied, "It's difficult to deal equally with a state party, with a sophisticated army, with the sort of army Israel has, with an air force, and a navy, and the most sophisticated weapons that are not only in the arsenal of Israel, but manufactured and exported by Israel, on the one hand, with Hamas using really improvised, imprecise armaments."[14] Although powerless beside Israeli armed might, Palestinians are often taken to task for not embracing a Gandhian strategy of nonviolent resistance. In 2003, then-US Deputy Secretary of Defense Paul Wolfowitz told a Georgetown University audience, "If the Palestinians would adopt the ways of Gandhi,

I think they could in fact make enormous change very, very quickly."[15] Whatever the merits of this contention, it should still be recalled what Gandhi actually had to say on the subject of nonviolence. He categorized forceful resistance in the face of impossible odds—a woman fending off a rapist with slaps and scratches, an unarmed man physically resisting torture by a gang, or Polish armed self-defense to the Nazi aggression—as "almost nonviolence" because it was essentially symbolic and a fillip to the spirit to overcome fear and enable a dignified death; it registered "a refusal to bend before overwhelming might in the full knowledge that it means certain death."[16] In the face of Israel's infernal, high-tech slaughter in Gaza, it is hard not to see desultory Hamas rocket attacks falling into the category of token violence that Gandhi was loath to condemn. Even if it were granted that Hamas rocket attacks did constitute full-fledged violence, it is still not certain that Gandhi would have disapproved. "Fight violence with nonviolence if you can," he counseled, "and if you can't do that, fight violence by any means, even if it means your utter extinction. But in no case should you leave your hearths and homes to be looted and burnt."[17] After Israel breached the cease-fire agreement and intensified the illegal blockade that was destroying Gaza's "whole civilization" (Mary Robinson) and causing "the breakdown of an entire society" (Sara Roy),[18] did Hamas really transgress the Mahatma's teachings when it decided to "fight violence by any means" even if it meant "utter extinction"?

The Goldstone Report did not limit itself narrowly to Cast Lead. It broadened out into a comprehensive, full-blown indictment of Israel's treatment of Palestinians during the long years of occupation. The Report condemned Israel's fragmentation of the Palestinian people,[19] and its restrictions on Palestinian freedom of movement and access;[20] its "institutionalized discrimination" against Palestinians both in the Occupied Palestinian Territories and in Israel;[21] its violent repression of Palestinian (as well as Israeli) demonstrators opposing the occupation, and the violent assaults on Palestinian civilians in the West Bank by Israeli soldiers and Jewish settlers;[22] its wholesale detention on political grounds of Palestinians (including hundreds of children as well as Hamas parliamentary members),[23] the lack of due process, and the violence inflicted on Palestinian detainees;[24] its "silent transfer" of Palestinians in East Jerusalem to ethnically cleanse it;[25] its "de facto annexation" of ten percent of the West Bank, which "amount[s] to the acquisition of territory by force, contrary to the Charter of the United Nations,"[26] and its settlement expansion, land expropriation, and demolition of Palestinian homes and villages. The Report concluded that certain of these policies constituted war crimes,[27] and also violated the "*jus cogens*" right (i.e., peremptory norm under international law) to self-determination.[28]

Although it did not mark out a clear distinction between those perpetrating and those resisting a brutal occupation, the Goldstone Report did not pretend to a false equivalence between Israel and the Palestinians either. On the contrary, it eschewed "equating the position of Israel as the Occupying Power with that of the occupied Palestinian population or entities representing it. The differences with regard to the power and capacity to inflict harm or to protect, including by securing justice when violations occur, are obvious."[29]

The Goldstone Report proposed several options to hold Israel and Gaza authorities accountable for violations of international law during Cast Lead. Individual states in the international community should "start criminal investigations in national courts, using univer-sal jurisdiction, where there is sufficient evidence of the commission of grave breaches of the Geneva Conventions of 1949. Where so warranted following investigation, alleged perpetrators should be arrested and prosecuted in accordance with internationally recognized standards of justice."[30] It also called on the UN Security Council to monitor the readiness of Israel and Gaza authorities to "launch appropriate investigations that are independent and in conformity with international standards into the serious violations of international humanitarian and international human rights law." If Israel and Gaza authorities failed to undertake "good-faith investiga-tions," the Goldstone Report recommended that the Security Council should "refer the situation in Gaza to the Prosecutor of the International Criminal Court."[31] It further recommended that Israel pay compensation for damages through a UN General Assembly escrow fund.[32]

Additionally, the Goldstone Report recommended that the High Contracting Parties to the Fourth Geneva Convention should convene in order to "enforce the Convention" and "ensure its respect" in the Occupied Palestinian Territories; that Israel terminate its blockade of Gaza and strangulation of Gaza's economy, its violence against Palestinian civilians, its "destruction and affronts on human dignity," its interference in Palestinian political life and repression of political dissent, and its restrictions on freedom of movement; that Palestinian armed groups "renounc[e] attacks on Israeli civilians and civilian objects" and release an Israeli soldier held in captivity; and that Palestinian authorities release political detainees and respect human rights.[33]

The Israeli reaction to the Goldstone Report came fast and furious. Apart from a few honorable (if predictable) exceptions,[34] it was subjected for months to a torrent of abuse across the Israeli political spectrum and at all levels of society. After ridiculing the Report as a "mockery of history," and Goldstone himself as a "small man, devoid of any sense of justice, a technocrat with no real understanding of jurisprudence," Israeli President Shimon Peres proceeded to set the record straight: "IDF [Israel Defense Forces] operations enabled economic prosperity in the West Bank, relieved southern Lebanese citizens from the terror of Hezbollah, and have enabled Gazans to have normal lives again."[35] Prime Minister Benjamin Netanyahu purported that the Goldstone Report was "a kangaroo court against Israel,"[36] while Defense Minister Ehud Barak inveighed that it was "a lie, distorted, biased and supports terror."[37] Netanyahu subsequently proposed launching an international campaign to "amend the rules of war" in order to facilitate the "battle against terrorists" in the future. ("What is it that Israel wants?," Israeli historian Zeev Sternhell wondered aloud. "Permission to fearlessly attack defenseless population centers with planes, tanks and artillery?")[38] Knesset Speaker Reuven Rivlin warned that the Goldstone Report's "new and crooked morality will usher in a new era in Western civilization, similar to the one that we remember from the [1938] Munich agreement."[39]

Ex-Foreign Minister Tzipi Livni declared that the Goldstone Report was "born in sin,"[40] while current Foreign Minister Avigdor Lieberman declared that it had "no legal, factual or moral value," and current Deputy Foreign Minister Danny Ayalon warned that it "provides legitimacy to terrorism" and risks "turning international law into a circus."[41] Israeli ambassador to the United States and ballyhooed historian Michael Oren intoned in the *Boston Globe* that the Goldstone Report "must be rebuffed by all those who care about peace"; alleged in an address to the American Jewish Committee that Hezbollah was one of the Report's prime beneficiaries; and reckoned in the *New Republic* that the Report was even worse than "[Iranian President Mahmoud] Ahmadinejad and the Holocaust deniers."[42]

Settler movement leader Israel Harel deemed the Goldstone Report "destructive, toxic," more wretched than the *Protocols of the Elders of Zion,* and misdirected "against precisely that country which protects human and military ethics more than the world has ever seen," while residents of Sderot picketed UN offices in Jerusalem holding placards that exhorted Goldstone to "apologize" and decried "anti-Semites."[43] A Tel Aviv University center for the study of "antisemitism and racism" alleged that the Goldstone Report was responsible for a global upsurge in "hate crimes against Jews" and "the equation of the war in Gaza with the Holocaust."[44] Fully 94 percent of Israeli Jews who were familiar with the Report's content held it to be biased against Israel, and 79 percent rejected its accusation that the IDF committed war crimes.[45] Since the Report's findings were beyond the pale, the only topic deemed worthy of deliberation in Israel was whether it had been prudent for Israel to boycott the Goldstone Mission.[46] But, as veteran peace activist Uri Avnery pointed out, the "real answer" as to why Israel chose not to cooperate "is quite simple: they knew full well that the mission, any mission, would have to reach the conclusions it did reach."[47]

Back in the US, the usual suspects rose (or sunk) to the occasion of smearing the message and the messenger. Elie Wiesel condemned the Goldstone Report as not only "a crime against the Jewish people" but also "unnecessary," ostensibly because "I can't believe that Israeli soldiers murdered people or shot children. It just can't be."[48] Harvard's Alan M. Dershowitz alleged that the Goldstone Report "is so filled with lies, distortions and blood libels that it could have been drafted by Hamas extremists"; that it recalled the *Protocols of the Elders of Zion* and was "biased and bigoted"; that "every serious student of human rights should be appalled at this anti-human rights and highly politicized report"; that it made "findings of fact (nearly all wrong)," stated "conclusions of law (nearly all questionable)," and made "specific recommendations (nearly all one-sided)"; and that Gold-stone himself was "a traitor to the Jewish people," an "evil, evil man" and—he said on Israeli television—on a par with Auschwitz "Angel of Death" Josef Mengele.[49]

The "essence" and "central conclusion" of the Goldstone Report, according to Dershowitz, was that Israel had a "carefully planned and executed policy of deliberately targeting innocent civilians for mass mur-der"; that Israel's "real purpose" was "to target inno-cent Palestinian civilians—children, women and the elderly—for death." He repeated this characterization of the Goldstone Report on nearly every page—often multiple times on a single page—of his lengthy "study in evidentiary bias," and then handily refuted the alle-gation.[50] The problem was that Dershowitz conjured a straw man: the Goldstone Report never said or implied that the principal objective of Cast Lead was to murder Palestinians. If the Goldstone Report did level such an allegation, it would have had to charge Israel with geno-cide—but it didn't. It is a commonplace that the more frequently a lie is repeated the more credible it becomes. The novelty of Dershowitz's "study" was that it kept repeating a lie, the more easily to discredit its purveyor.

Dershowitz and other Goldstone-bashers also alleged that Palestinian witnesses were either coached and intimidated by Hamas or were actually Hamas militants in disguise, without a jot of evidence being adduced,[51] while Goldstone himself emphatically rejoined that "it didn't happen."[52]

The American Israel Public Affairs Committee (AIPAC) called the Goldstone Mission "rigged" and the Goldstone Report "deeply flawed,"[53] the American Jewish Committee deplored it as a "deeply distorted document,"[54] and Abraham Foxman of the Anti-Defamation League was "shocked and distressed that the United States would not unilaterally dismiss it."[55] New York Democrat Gary Ackerman, chair of the House Subcommittee on the Middle East and South Asia, mocked Goldstone as inhabiting a "self-righteous fantasyland" and the Report as a "pompous, tendentious, one-sided political diatribe."[56] The US House of Representatives passed by a vote of 344 to 36 a nonbinding resolution that condemned the Goldstone Report as "irredeemably biased and unworthy of further consideration or legitimacy."[57] Before the vote was taken, Goldstone provided a point-by-point demonstration that the House resolution was vitiated by "serious factual inaccuracies and instances where information and statements are taken grossly out of context."[58]

The Obama administration quickly fell into line with the Israel lobby, but it probably did not need much prodding. An Israeli talking point in Washington was that the Goldstone Report's recommendation to prosecute soldiers for war crimes "should worry every country fighting terror."[59] In its 47-page entry for "Israel and the occupied territories," the US State Department's *2009 Human Rights Report* devoted all of three sentences to Cast Lead, then touched on the Goldstone Mission's findings and dismissively concluded: "The Goldstone report was widely criticized for methodological failings, legal and factual errors, falsehoods, and for devoting insufficient attention to the asymmetrical nature of the conflict and the fact that Hamas and other Palestinian militants were deliberately operating in heavily populated urban areas of Gaza."[60] After enduring a barrage of such attacks, Goldstone finally challenged the Obama administration to justify substantively its criticism of the Report, while Human Rights Watch (HRW) took to task the US government for having "resorted to calling the report 'unbalanced' and 'deeply flawed,' but providing no real facts to support those assertions."[61]

Meanwhile, Washington reportedly planned to block or limit UN Security Council action on the Goldstone Report, while both the US and Israel pressured the Palestinian Authority (PA) to drop its support of the Report's recommendations. "The PA has reached the point where it has to decide," a senior Israeli defense official pronounced, "whether it is working with us or against us."[62] The answer was not long in coming. Acting on direct instructions from President Mahmoud Abbas, the PA representative on the UN Human Rights Council effectively acquiesced in killing consideration of the Goldstone Report. However, the decision evoked such outrage among Palestinians that the PA was forced to reverse itself and the council convened to consider the Report's findings.[63] It approved a resolution "condemning all targeting of civilians and stressing the urgent need to ensure accountability for all violations" of international law, and it endorsed the Report's recommendations and urged the UN to act on them.[64] In November 2009, the UN General Assembly passed by a vote of 114 to 18 (44 countries abstained) a resolution also "condemning all targeting of civilians and civilian infrastructure," and it called on both Israel and the "Palestinian side" to "undertake investigations that are independent, credible and in conformity with international standards into the serious violations of international . . . law reported by the Fact-Finding Mission."[65] Israeli officials denounced the resolution as "completely detached from realities" and a "mockery of reality."[66]

In February 2010, UN Secretary-General Ban Ki-moon reported back to the General Assembly that as yet "no determination can be made on the implementation" of its November 2009 resolution calling for credible investigations.[67] Later in the month, the General Assembly passed another resolution by a vote of 98 to 7 (31 countries abstained) reiterating its call on Israel and Hamas to "conduct investigations that are independent, credible and in conformity with international standards," and requesting that the Secretary-General report back within five months on the implementation of the resolution.[68] Despite intensive lobbying by European Jewish groups, the European Parliament passed in March 2010 by a vote of 335 to 287 a resolution "demanding" implementation of the Goldstone Report's recommendations and "accountability for all violations of international law, including alleged war crimes." The spokesman for the Israeli mission to the European Union deplored the resolution as "flawed and counterproductive."[69]

In January and July 2010, Israel released "updates" on its own investigations.[70] Although it purportedly conducted scores of inquiries, the results overwhelmingly exonerated Israelis of wrongdoing. A handful of soldiers suffered disciplinary sanctions, such as an officer who was "severely reprimanded." The one and only Israeli convicted on a criminal charge and sentenced to prison was a soldier who stole a credit card.[71] Even these risibly token punishments evoked indignation in IDF ranks.[72] Still, the Israeli investigations could not be faulted for lack of creativity. One soldier who killed a woman carrying a white flag was exonerated on the grounds that the bullet was actually a "warning shot" that "ricocheted"[73]—off a cloud? Despite near-total vindication by these "investigations," in a magnanimous gesture Israel "adopted important new written procedures and doctrine designed to enhance the protection of civilians . . . and to limit unnecessary damage to civilian property and infrastructure" in future conflicts[74]—as if the death and destruction in Gaza had resulted from operational and doctrinal deficits and not from an assault expressly designed to "punish, humiliate and terrorize a civilian population."[75]

The UN High Commissioner for Human Rights announced in June 2010 the formation of an independent panel to "ensure accountability for all violations of international humanitarian and international human rights laws during the Gaza conflict."[76] The committee was chaired by a former member of the International Law Commission and included a former Justice of the Supreme Court of the State of New York. The committee's report, issued in September 2010,[77] found that, although "certain positive steps . . . have resulted from Israel's investigations," the bottom line was that "the military investigations thus far appear to have produced very little."[78] Indeed, while "the Committee cannot conclude that credible and genuine investigations have been carried out by the de facto authorities in the Gaza Strip,"[79] Hamas had apparently convicted and sentenced to prison time more individuals than Israel.[80] After release of this report, Amnesty International urged the UN Human Rights Council to "recognize the failure of the investigations conducted by Israel and the Hamas de facto administration," and to "call on the ICC [International Criminal Court] Prosecutor urgently to seek a determination . . . whether the ICC has jurisdiction over the Gaza conflict."[81]

One might wonder why the Goldstone Report should have triggered so much vituperation in Israel and set off an Israeli "diplomatic blitz" to contain the fallout from it.[82] After all, the Goldstone Mission's findings were merely the last in a long series of human rights reports condemning Israeli actions in Gaza,[83] and Israel has never been known for its deference to UN bodies. The answer, however, is not hard to find. Goldstone is not only Jewish but also a self-declared "Zionist" who "worked for Israel all of my adult life," "fully support[s] Israel's right to exist" and is a "firm believer in the absolute right of the Jewish people to have their home there." He headed up a Jewish organization that runs vocational schools in Israel and sits on the Board of Governors of the Hebrew University in Jerusalem (from which he also received an honorary doctorate). Moreover, his mother was an activist in the women's

Zionist movement, and his daughter made *aliyah* (Zionist emigration to Israel) and remains an ardent Zionist.[84] Goldstone has also claimed the Nazi holocaust as the seminal inspiration for the international law and human rights agenda of which he is a leading exponent.[85]

Because of Goldstone's pedigree and bona fides, Israel could not credibly play its usual cards—"anti-Semite," "self-hating Jew," "Holocaust denier"—against him. In effect, his persona neutralized the ideological weapons Israel had honed over many years to ward off criticism. Soon the detractors started speculating that the Goldstone Report was a product of the author's overweening ambition—Goldstone was supposedly angling for a Nobel Peace Prize or to head the United Nations—but once more his impeccable reputation easily withstood the imputations.[86] It was then alleged that Goldstone had been "suckered into lending his good name to a half-baked report."[87] But the chief prosecutor in multiple international war crimes tribunals was plainly no one's dupe. If Goldstone was not an anti-Semite, a self-hating Jew, or a Holocaust denier; if he had never evinced animus towards Israel but in fact had demonstrated an abiding affection for it; if he was manifestly a man of integrity who put truth and justice above self-aggrandizement and partisanship; if he was neither an incompetent nor a fool; then the only plausible explanation for the devastating content of the document he coauthored was that it faithfully recorded the facts as they unfolded during the 22-day invasion. "The only thing they can be afraid of," Goldstone later observed, "is the truth. And I think this is why they're attacking the messenger and not the message."[88]

Compelled to face the facts and their consequences, disarmed and exposed, Israel went into panic mode. Influential Israeli columnists expressed alarm that the Goldstone Report might impede Israel's ability to launch military attacks in the future,[89] and Prime Minister Netanyahu ranked "the Iranian [nuclear] threat, the missile threat and a threat I call the Goldstone threat" the major strategic challenges confronting Israel.[90] In the meantime, Israeli officials fretted that prosecutors might hound Israelis traveling abroad.[91] And indeed, shortly after the Goldstone Report was released, the International Criminal Court announced that it was contemplating an investigation of an Israeli officer implicated in the Gaza massacre.[92] Then, in December 2009,

Tzipi Livni cancelled a trip to London after a British court issued an arrest warrant for her role in the commission of war crimes while serving as foreign minister and member of the war cabinet during Cast Lead. In June 2010, two Belgian lawyers representing a group of Palestinians charged 14 Israeli politicians (including Livni and Barak) with committing crimes against humanity and war crimes during the invasion.[93]

The symbolism, indeed pathos, of Goldstone's condemnation of Israel was hard to miss. A lover of Zion was now calling for Zion to be hauled before the International Criminal Court for an array of war crimes and possible crimes against humanity. It can fairly be said that the Goldstone Report marked the end of one era and the emergence of another: the end of an apologetic Jewish liberalism that denies or extenuates Israel's crimes and the emergence of a Jewish liberalism that returns to its classical calling that, if only as an ideal imperfectly realized, nonetheless holds all malefactors, Jew or non-Jew, accountable when they have strayed from the path of justice.

In order to discredit or, at least, undercut the Goldstone Report, Israel had reached into the utter depths of its state and society, harnessing and concentrating their full forces, and mobilized the Jewish state's faithful appa-ratchiks abroad. Nonetheless, months after it was pub-lished an Israeli columnist rued, "the Goldstone Report still holds the top spot in the bestseller list of Israel's headaches."[94]

3/ WE KNOW A LOT MORE TODAY (2011)

ON 1 APRIL 2011, ISRAEL'S BIGGEST HEADACHE finally went away. Dropping a bombshell on the op-ed page of the *Washington Post*,[1] Richard Goldstone effectively disowned the devastating UN report of Israeli crimes carrying his name.[2]

Israel was jubilant. "Everything that we said proved to be true," Prime Minister Benjamin Netanyahu crowed. "We always said that the IDF [Israel Defense Forces] is a moral army that acted according to international law," Defense Minister Ehud Barak declared. "We had no doubt that the truth would come out eventually," Foreign Minister Avigdor Lieberman proclaimed.[3] The Obama administration used the occasion of Goldstone's recantation to affirm that Israel had not "engaged in any war crimes" during Operation Cast Lead, while the US Senate unanimously called on the United Nations to "rescind" the Goldstone Report.[4]

Some commentators have endeavored to prove by parsing his words that Goldstone did not actually recant. While this might technically be true, such a rhetorical strategy will not wash. Goldstone is a distinguished jurist. He knows how to use precise language. If he did not want to sever his connection with the Report, he could simply have said, "I am not recanting my original report by which I still stand." He must have known exactly how his words would be spun, and it is this fallout—not his parsed words—that we must now confront.

Goldstone has done terrible damage to the cause of truth and justice and the rule of law. He has poisoned Jewish-Palestinian relations, undermined the courageous work of Israeli dissenters and—most unforgivably—increased the risk of another merciless IDF assault. There has been much speculation on why Goldstone recanted. Was he blackmailed? Did he finally succumb to the relentless hate campaign directed against him? Did he decide to put his tribe ahead of truth? What can be said with certainty is that *Goldstone did not reverse himself on account of newly unearthed information.*

Goldstone justifies his recantation on the grounds that "we know a lot more today about what happened" during Cast Lead than when the Mission compiled the Report. On the basis of this alleged new information, he suggests that Israel did not commit war crimes in Gaza and that Israel is fully capable on its own of investigating violations of international law that did occur. It is correct that much new information on what happened has become available since publication of the Goldstone Report. But the vast preponderance of this new material sustains and even extends the Report's findings.

Many Israeli combatants stepped forward after release of the Goldstone Report and testified to the invasion's brutality. For example, an officer who served at a brigade headquarters recalled that IDF policy amounted to ensuring "literally zero risk to the soldiers," while a combatant remembered a meeting with his brigade commander and others where it was conveyed that "if you see any signs of movement at all you shoot. This is essentially the rules of engagement."[5] Goldstone could have cited this new information to buttress his Report; instead, he chose to ignore it. In 2010, Human Rights Watch published a report based on satellite imagery documenting numerous cases "in which Israeli forces caused extensive destruction of homes, factories, farms and greenhouses in areas under IDF control without any evident military purpose. These cases occurred when there was no fighting in these areas; in many cases, the destruction was carried out during the final days of the campaign when an Israeli withdrawal was imminent."[6] Goldstone could have cited this new information to buttress his Report; instead, he again chose to ignore it.

How is it possible to take seriously Goldstone's claim that the facts compelled him to recant when he scrupulously ignores the copious new evidence confirming his Report?

Since publication of the Goldstone Report, Israel has released many purported refutations of it. The most voluminous of these was a 350-page report compiled by the Israeli Intelligence and Terrorism Information Center in 2010. The Israeli document was based on unverifiable "reports from IDF forces" and "Israeli intelligence information," indecipherable photographic evidence and information gathered from "terrorist operatives" who had almost certainly been tortured. It falsely alleged that the Goldstone Report made "almost no mention of the brutal means of repression used by Hamas against its opponents"; that the Goldstone Report devoted "just three paragraphs" to Hamas's "rocket and mortar fire" during the Israeli invasion; that the Goldstone Report "absolved" Hamas "of all responsibility for war crimes"; that the Goldstone Report gave "superficial" treatment to "the terrorist organizations' use of civilians as human shields"; and that the Goldstone Report depended on "the unreliable casualty statistics provided by Hamas."[7] One is hard-pressed to reconcile the mendacity of Israel's most ambitious attempt to refute the Goldstone Report with Goldstone's claim that new Israeli information fatally undermines the Report.

The heart of Goldstone's recantation is that, on the basis of new information, he has concluded that "civilians were not intentionally targeted as a matter of policy." It is not entirely clear what is being asserted here. If Goldstone is saying that he no longer believes Israel had a *systematic policy* of targeting Gaza's civilian population *for murder*, his recantation is gratuitous: the Goldstone Report never made such a claim. If the Report had leveled such an accusation, it would have been tantamount to charging Israel with genocide. But the Report never even came close to entertaining, let alone leveling, such a charge. What the Goldstone Report did say was that Cast Lead was a "deliberately disproportionate attack designed to punish, humiliate and terrorize a civilian population." In fact, the Goldstone Report assembles compelling evidence that, as a matter of policy, Israel resorted to indiscriminate, disproportionate force against the civilian population of Gaza. Goldstone does not allege in his *Washington Post* op-ed that new information calls this evidence into doubt.

Israeli leaders themselves did not shy away from acknowledging the indiscriminate, disproportionate nature of the attack they launched. As the invasion wound down, Foreign Minister Tzipi Livni declared that it had "restored Israel's deterrence . . . Hamas now understands that when you fire on [Israel's] citizens it responds by going wild—and this is a good thing." The day after the cease-fire, Livni bragged on Israeli television, "Israel demonstrated real hooliganism during the course of the recent operation, which I demanded."[8] A former Israeli defense official told the Crisis Group that "with an armada of fighter planes attacking Gaza, Israel decided to play the role of a mad dog for the sake of future deterrence," while a former senior Israeli security official boasted to the Crisis Group that Israel had regained its deterrence because it "has shown Hamas, Iran and the region that it can be as lunatic as any of them."[9] "The Goldstone Report, which claimed that Israel goes crazy when it is being attacked, caused us some damage," a leading Israeli commentator on Arab affairs observed, "yet it was a blessing in our region. If Israel goes crazy and destroys everything in its way when it is being attacked, one should be careful. No need to mess with crazy people."[10]

It is a tenet of law that "the doer of an act must be taken to have *intended* its natural and foreseeable consequences."[11] Thus, an indiscriminate, disproportionate attack that inevitably and predictably results in civilian deaths is indistinguishable from a deliberate and intentional attack on civilians. "There is no genuine difference between a premeditated attack against civilians (or civilian objects) and a reckless disregard of the principle of distinction" between civilians (or civilian objects) and combatants (or military objects), according to Yoram Dinstein, Israel's leading authority on international law—"they are equally forbidden."[12] If Goldstone now believes that because Israel did not intentionally target civilians, it is not guilty of war crimes, he ought to brush up on the law: an indiscriminate, disproportionate attack on civilian areas is no less criminal than deliberately targeting them. If he now believes that it is not criminal behavior for an invading army to go "wild," demonstrate "real hooliganism," carry on like a "mad dog," act "lunatic" and "crazy," and "destroy everything in its way," then he should not be practicing law.

To sustain his implicit contention that Israel did not commit *any* war crimes because it *never* targeted civilians, Goldstone revisits the notorious case of the al-Samouni family. It merits juxtaposing his 1 April 2011 account in the *Washington Post* of what a new Israeli investigation allegedly shows with the account he himself gave at a Stanford University forum two months earlier,[13] the account of Amnesty International in March 2011,[14] and the account of a March 2011 UN report that he himself praises.[15] Goldstone's critical omissions are highlighted below:

GOLDSTONE, 1 APRIL 2011:

[T]he most serious attack the Goldstone Report focused on was the killing of some 29 members of the al-Simouni [*sic*] family in their home. The shelling of the home was apparently the

consequence of an Israeli commander's errone-
ous interpretation of a drone image.

GOLDSTONE AT STANFORD, TWO MONTHS EARLIER:
[T]he single most serious incident reported in the
[Goldstone] Report—[was] the bombing of the
home of the al-Samouni family.... On January
4, 2009, members of the Givati Brigade of **the
IDF decided to take over the house of Saleh
al-Samouni as part of the IDF ground operation; they ordered its occupants to relocate to
the home of Wa'el al-Samouni. It was located
about 35 yards away and within sight of the
Israeli soldiers.... In the result there were
over 100 members of the family gathered in
the single story home of Wa'el al-Samouni.
Early on the cold wintry morning of 5 January, several male members of the al-Samouni
family went outside to gather firewood. They
were in clear sight of the Israeli troops.** As the
men returned with the firewood, projectiles fired
from helicopter gunships killed or injured them.
Immediately after that further projectiles hit the

house. Twenty-one members of the family were killed, some of them young children and women. Nineteen were injured. Of those injured, another eight subsequently died from their injuries. . . . [This evidence] led the Fact-Finding Mission to conclude that, as a probability, the attack on the al-Samouni family constituted a deliberate attack on civilians. The crucial consideration was that **the men, women and children were known by the Israeli troops to be civilians and were ordered by them to relocate to a house that was in the vicinity of their command post. Members of the al-Samouni family had regarded the presence of the IDF as a guarantee of their safety**. . . . [A]t the end of October 2010 (almost 22 months after the incident), to the credit of the Israeli Military Police, they announced that they were investigating whether the air strike against the al-Samouni home was authorized by a senior Givati brigade commander who had been warned of the danger to civilians. At about the same time there were reports that the attack followed upon the receipt of photographs by the Israeli military from a drone showing what was incorrectly interpreted to be a group of men carrying rocket launchers towards a house. The order was given to bomb the men and the building. According to these reports, the photograph received from the drone was not of high quality and in fact showed the men carrying firewood to the al-Samouni home. The results of this military police investigation are as yet unknown.

AMNESTY INTERNATIONAL, MARCH 2011:

One prominent case that was examined by the [Goldstone Mission] and various human rights groups and is the subject of an ongoing Israeli criminal investigation is the killing of some 21 members of the al-Sammouni family, who were sheltering in the home of Wa'el al-Sammouni when it was struck by missiles or shells on 5 January 2009. The Israeli military announced that an MPCID [Military Police Criminal Investigations Division] investigation had been opened into this incident on 6 July 2010. On 21 October 2010, Colonel Ilan Malka, who was commander of the Givati Brigade . . . and was allegedly involved in approving the air strike which killed

21 members of the al-Sammouni family, was questioned under caution by military police. According to media reports, he claimed that he was unaware of the presence of civilians in the building when he approved the strike. **The decision to approve the air strike was reportedly based on drone photographs of men from the al-Sammouni family breaking apart boards for firewood; the photographs were interpreted in the war room as Palestinians armed with rocket-propelled grenades. But at the time the photographs were received, the family had already been confined to the building and surrounded and observed by soldiers from the Givati Brigade in at least six different nearby outposts for more than 24 hours; at least some soldiers in these outposts would have known that the family were civilians since they themselves had ordered the family to gather in Wa'el al-Sammouni's home. Some of these officers reportedly testified to the military investigators that they had warned Colonel Malka that there could be civilians in the area.**
[endnotes omitted]

UN COMMITTEE REPORT, MARCH 2011:

The Committee does not have sufficient information to establish the current status of the ongoing criminal investigations into the killings of Ateya and Ahmad Samouni, the attack on the Wa'el al-Samouni house and the shooting of Iyad Samouni. This is of considerable concern: reportedly 24 civilians were killed and 19 were injured in the related incidents on 4 and 5 January 2009. Furthermore, the events may relate both to the actions and decisions of soldiers on the ground and of senior officers located in a war room, as well as to broader issues implicating the rules of engagement and the use of drones.... Media reports further inform that **a senior officer, who was questioned "under caution" and had his promotion put on hold, told investigators that he was not warned that civilians were at the location. However, some of those civilians had been ordered there by IDF soldiers from that same officer's unit and air force officers reportedly informed him of the possible presence of civilians. Despite allegedly being made aware**

of this information, the officer apparently approved air strikes that killed 21 people and injured 19 gathered in the al-Samouni house. Media sources also report that the incident has been described as a legitimate interpretation of drone photographs portrayed on a screen and that the special command investigation, initiated ten months after the incidents, did not conclude that there had been anything out of the ordinary in the strike. [endnotes omitted]

In his recantation, Goldstone excised all the evidence casting doubt on the new Israeli alibi. His tendentious depiction of the facts might be appropriate if he were Israel's defense attorney, but it hardly befits the head of a mission that was mandated to ferret out the truth.

Goldstone justifies his about-face on the grounds that "we know a lot more today." It is unclear, however, what, if anything, "a lot more" consists of. He points to the findings of Israeli military investigations. But what do "we know . . . today" about these in camera hearings except what Israel says about them? In fact, Israel has furnished virtually no information on which to independently

assess the evidence adduced or the fairness of these proceedings. It is not even known how many investigations
are complete and how many still ongoing.[16]

Although he claims to "know a lot more," and bases
his recantation on this "a lot more," neither Goldstone
nor anyone else could have independently assessed any
of this purportedly new information before he recanted.
Even in the three investigations that resulted in criminal
indictments, the proceedings were often inaccessible to
the public (apart from the indicted soldiers' supporters)
and full transcripts of the proceedings were not made
publicly available.[17] It's certain, however, that no information coming out of these criminal indictments could
have caused Goldstone to *reverse* himself; if anything,
they buttressed his original Report.

The key example of revelatory new information Goldstone cites is the drone image. The misreading of it, Israel
alleges (and Goldstone tentatively assents), caused an officer to mistakenly target an extended family of civilians. If,
as humanitarian and human rights organizations declared
right after the al-Samouni killings, it was one of the "grav-
est" and "most shocking" incidents[18] of the Israeli assault,
and if, as Goldstone said, the al-Samouni killings were "the

single most serious incident" in his Report, then the wonder
is that Israel did not rush to restore its bruised reputation
after Cast Lead but instead waited *22 months* before coming
forth with so simple an explanation. To defend itself against
Goldstone's findings, Israel disseminated numerous aerial
photographs taken during the Gaza assault. Why has Israel
still not made publicly available this drone image that
allegedly exonerates it of criminal culpability for the most
egregious incident of which it was accused? It is also cause
for wonder why Goldstone credits this new Israeli "evidence" sight unseen, yet ignores genuinely new evidence
revealed by Israeli journalist Amira Hass in *Haaretz* after
his Report's publication: that before the attack—the civilian
deaths of which allegedly surprised the Givati brigade commander who ordered it—"a Givati force set up outposts and
bases in at least six houses in the Samouni compound."[19]
Didn't the Givati commander check with these soldiers
on the ground before launching the murderous attack, to
ascertain that they were out of harm's way? Didn't he ask
them whether they had observed men carrying rocket
launchers, and didn't they reply no?

Israel might be able to furnish plausible answers in
its defense. But Goldstone does not even bother to pose

these obvious questions because "we know ... today"—
Israel said so—it was just a simple mistake. After publication of the Goldstone Report, Israeli authorities had a
ready-made, if evidence-free, explanation not just for the
al-Samouni killings but also for many of the other documented war crimes. They alleged that the al-Bader flour
mill was destroyed "in order to neutralize immediate
threats to IDF forces";[20] that the Sawafeary chicken farm
had been destroyed "for reasons of military necessity";[21]
and that the al-Maqadmah mosque was targeted because
"two terrorist operatives [were] standing near the
entrance."[22] Do "we know ... today" that the copious evidence of war crimes assembled in the Goldstone Report
and thousands of pages of other human rights reports
was all wrong just because Israel says so? Did we also
"know" during Cast Lead that Israel wasn't using white
phosphorus because it emphatically denied such use?

The only other scrap of novel information Goldstone
references in his recantation is a revised casualty figure
belatedly announced by a Hamas official. On the basis of
this new reckoning, Goldstone observes, the number of
Hamas combatants killed during Cast Lead "turned out
to be similar" to the official Israeli figure. The upshot is,

Hamas's figure appeared to confirm Israel's contention that combatants, not civilians, comprised the majority of Gazans killed during the invasion. But then Goldstone notes parenthetically that Hamas "may have reason to inflate" its figure. So why does he credit it?

To prove that it defeated Israel on the battlefield, Hamas originally alleged that only 48 of its fighters had been killed. After the full breadth of Israel's destruction became apparent and the claims of a battlefield victory rang hollow, and in the face of accusations that the people of Gaza "had paid the price" of its reckless decisions, Hamas abruptly upped the figure by several hundred in order to show that it, too, had suffered major losses.[23] As none other than Goldstone himself put it at Stanford just two months before his recantation, the new Hamas figure "was intended to bolster the reputation of Hamas with the people of Gaza."[24] Whereas Goldstone now defers to this politically inflated Hamas figure, the Goldstone Report relied on numbers furnished by respected Israeli and Palestinian human rights organizations, each of which independently and meticulously investigated the aggregate and civilian/combatant breakdown of those killed. Disputing Israel's claim that only 300 Gazan civilians were killed,[25] these human rights organizations put the figure at some 800–1,200[26] and also demonstrated that Israeli figures lacked credibility.[27] Even the largely apologetic US Department of State *2009 Human Rights Report* put the number of dead "at close to 1,400 Palestinians, including more than 1,000 civilians."[28] But because a politically manipulated Israeli figure chimes with a politically manipulated Hamas figure, Goldstone discards the much larger figure for Palestinian civilian deaths documented by human rights organizations and even validated by the US State Department.

In his recantation, Goldstone avows that he is "confident" Israeli military investigations will bring those guilty of wrongdoing to justice. He goes on to assert that Israel has already "done this to a significant degree." In fact, in this instance we *do* have new data since publication of the Goldstone Report but, alas, they hardly redeem his newfound faith. In the course of Cast Lead, Israel damaged or destroyed "everything in its way," including 280 schools and kindergartens, 1,500 factories and workshops, electrical, water and sewage installations, 190 greenhouse complexes, 80 percent of agricultural crops, and nearly one-fifth of cultivated land. Whole neighborhoods were laid waste; fully 600,000 tons of rubble were left behind after Israel withdrew. More than two years later, the only penalty Israel has imposed for unlawful property destruction was some disciplinary measure penalizing one soldier.[29] Yet Goldstone is now not only "confident" that Israeli wrongdoers will be punished, but also asserts that Israel has already "done this to a significant degree."

Beyond killing 1,400 Palestinians (including more than 300 children) and the massive destruction it inflicted on civilian infrastructure, Israel damaged or destroyed 29 ambulances, almost half of Gaza's 122 health facilities (including 15 hospitals), and 45 mosques. It also—in the words of Human Rights Watch—"repeatedly exploded white phosphorus munitions in the air over populated areas, killing and injuring civilians, and damaging civilian structures, including a school, a market, a humanitarian aid warehouse and a hospital."[30] Both the Goldstone Report and human rights organizations concluded that much of this death and destruction would constitute war crimes. More than two years later, the only Israeli soldier who did jail time for criminal conduct served seven months after being convicted of credit card theft. Yet Goldstone is now not only "confident" that

Israeli wrongdoers will be punished, but also asserts that Israel has already "done this to a significant degree."

To be sure, Israel did express remorse at what happened in Gaza. "I am ashamed of the soldier," Information Minister Yuli Edelstein declared, "who stole some credit cards."[31] After this wondrous show of contrition, how could Goldstone not be "confident" of Israel's resolve to punish wrongdoers?

In his recantation, Goldstone can barely contain his loathing and contempt for Hamas. He says that, unlike in Israel's case, Hamas's criminal intent "goes without saying—its rockets were purposefully and indiscriminately aimed at civilian targets." The Goldstone Report had reached this conclusion on the basis of a couple of statements by Hamas leaders combined with Hamas's actual targeting of these civilian areas. It is unclear, however, why comparable statements by Israeli officials combined with Israel's purposeful and indiscriminate targeting of civilian areas in Gaza no longer prove Israel's criminal guilt. In fact, judging by his Report's findings, none of which Goldstone repudiates, the case against Israel was incontrovertible. If, as Israel asserted and investigators found, it possessed fine "grid maps" of Gaza and an "intelligence gathering capacity" that "remained extremely effective"; and if it made extensive use of state-of-the-art precision weaponry; and if 99 percent of the Israeli Air Force's combat missions hit targets accurately; and if it only once targeted a building erroneously: then, as the Goldstone Report logically concluded, the massive destruction Israel inflicted on Gaza's civilian infrastructure must have "resulted from deliberate planning and policy decisions throughout the chain of command, down to the standard operating procedures and instructions given to the troops on the ground."[32]

It has "done nothing," Goldstone further chastises Hamas, to investigate the criminal conduct of Gazans during the Israeli invasion. Hamas attacks killed three Israeli civilians and nearly destroyed one civilian home. The Israeli assault on Gaza killed as many as 1,200 civilians and nearly or totally destroyed more than 6,000 civilian homes. Hamas did not sentence anyone to prison for criminal misconduct, according to Goldstone, whereas Israel sentenced one soldier to seven months prison time for stealing a credit card.[33] Isn't it blazingly obvious how much eviler Hamas is?

In his recantation, Goldstone declares that his goal is to apply evenhandedly the laws of war to state and non-state actors. It is unlikely however that this admirable objective will be advanced by his double standards. Goldstone now rues his "unrealistic" hope that Hamas would have investigated itself. Meanwhile, his detractors heap ridicule on his past naiveté: *How could a terrorist organization like Hamas have possibly investigated itself?* Only civilized countries like Israel are capable of such self-scrutiny. Indeed, Israel's judicial record precisely quantifies its capacity in this regard. The Israeli human rights organization B'Tselem found that, in the decade following the outbreak of the first intifada, 1,300 Palestinians had been killed yet only 19 Israeli soldiers were convicted of homicide, while the Israeli human rights organization Yesh Din found that, although thousands of Palestinian civilians were killed during the second intifada, only five Israeli soldiers were held criminally liable and not a single Israeli soldier was convicted on a murder or manslaughter charge.[34]

Goldstone plainly did not publish his recantation because "we know a lot more today." What he calls new information consists *entirely* of unverifiable assertions by parties with vested interests. The fact that he cannot cite any genuinely new evidence to justify his recantation is the most telling proof that none exists. What, then, happened? Ever since publication of his Report, Goldstone has been the object of a relentless smear campaign. Harvard professor Alan Dershowitz compared him to Auschwitz "Angel of Death" Josef Mengele, while the Israeli ambassador to the United States excoriated the Goldstone Report as even worse than "Ahmadinejad and the Holocaust deniers."[35] Goldstone was not the only one who came under attack. The UN Human Rights Council appointed the eminent international jurist Christian Tomuschat to chair a follow-up committee mandated to determine whether Israeli and Hamas officials were investigating the Goldstone Report's allegations. Deciding that Tomuschat was insufficiently pliant, the Israel lobby hounded and defamed him until he had no choice but to step down.[36]

Many aspects of Goldstone's recantation are perplexing.

Goldstone is reputed to be very ambitious.[37] Although he was savaged after publication of his Report, the tide began to turn in his favor this past year. In Israel, the newspaper *Haaretz* editorialized that it was "time to thank the critics for forcing the IDF to examine itself and amend its procedures. Even if not all of Richard Goldstone's 32 charges were solid and valid, some of them certainly were."[38] In the US, *Tikkun* magazine honored Goldstone at a gala 25th anniversary celebration. In South Africa, distinguished personalities, such as Judge Dennis Davis, formerly of the Jewish Board of Deputies, publicly denounced a visit by Alan Dershowitz because, among other things, he had "grossly misrepresented the judicial record of Judge Richard Goldstone."[39] It is puzzling why an ambitious jurist at the peak of a long and distinguished career would commit what might be professional suicide, alienating his colleagues in the human rights community and throwing doubt on his judicial temperament, just as his star was again on the rise.

Throughout his professional career, Goldstone has functioned in bureaucracies and has no doubt internalized their norms. Yet, in a shocking rupture with bureaucratic protocol, he dropped his bombshell without first

notifying his three colleagues on the original delegation
or anyone at the United Nations. Did Goldstone fear
confronting them beforehand because he knew that he
didn't have grounds to issue a recantation and could not
possibly defend it? If so, his worries proved well founded.
Shortly after publication of his recantation, all three
of Goldstone's colleagues—Christine Chinkin, Hina
Jilani and Desmond Travers—issued a joint statement
unequivocally affirming the Report's original findings:
"We concur in our view that there is no justification for
any demand or expectation for reconsideration of the
report as nothing of substance has appeared that would
in any way change the context, findings or conclusions of
that report."[40]

In his *Washington Post* op-ed, Goldstone alleges
that it was new information on the killings of the
al-Samouni family and the revised Hamas figure of
combatants killed that induced him to recant. But
just two months earlier at Stanford University he
matter-of-factly addressed these very same points
without drawing any dramatic conclusions. No new
evidence surfaced in the interim. In his recantation,
Goldstone also references a UN document in order to

issue Israel a clean bill of health on its investigations. But this document was much more critical of Israeli investigations than he lets on.[41] It is as if Goldstone were desperately clutching at any shred of evidence, however problematic, to justify his recantation. Indeed, he rushed to acquit Israel of criminal culpability in the al-Samouni deaths even before the Israeli military had completed its investigation.

A few days before submitting his op-ed to the *Washington Post*, Goldstone submitted another version of it to the *New York Times*.[42] The *Times* rejected the submission apparently because it did *not* repudiate the Goldstone Report. The impression one gets is of Goldstone being pressured against his will to publish a repudiation of his Report. To protect his reputation and because his heart is not in it, Goldstone submits a wishy-washy recantation to the *Times*. After the *Times* rejects it, and in a race against the clock, he hurriedly slips in wording that can be construed as a full-blown repudiation, thus ensuring that the *Post* will run what is now a bombshell. The exertion of outside pressure on Goldstone would perhaps also explain the murkiness of his op-ed, in which he seems to be simultaneously recanting and not recanting the

Report, and his embarrassing inclusion of irrelevances, such as a call on the Human Rights Council to condemn the slaughter of an Israeli settler family—two years after Cast Lead in an incident unrelated to the Gaza Strip—by unknown perpetrators.

The eminent South African jurist John Dugard is a colleague of Goldstone's. Dugard also headed a fact-finding mission that investigated Cast Lead. The conclusions of his report—which contained a finer legal analysis while Goldstone's was broader in scope—largely overlapped with those of the Goldstone Mission: "the purpose of Israel's action was to punish the people of Gaza," it said, adding that Israel was "responsible for the commission of internationally wrongful acts by reason of the commission of war crimes and crimes against humanity."[43] In a devastating dissection of Goldstone's recantation in the *New Statesman*, Dugard concluded: "There are no new facts that exonerate Israel and that could possibly have led Goldstone to change his mind. What made him change his mind therefore remains a closely guarded secret."[44] Although Goldstone's secret will perhaps never be revealed and his recantation has caused irreparable damage, it is still possible by patient reconstruction of the factual record to know the truth about what happened in Gaza. Out of respect for the memory of those who perished during Operation Cast Lead, we must preserve and protect this truth from its assassins.

4/ DANGEROUS AND RECKLESS ACT (2011)

THE MASSIVE DESTRUCTION Israel inflicted during Operation Cast Lead was designed in part to exacerbate the effects of its illegal and inhuman blockade. "I fully expected to see serious damage, but I have to say I was really shocked when I saw the extent and precision of the destruction," the World Food Program director for the Gaza Strip observed after the assault. "It was precisely the strategic economic areas that Gaza depends on to relieve its dependency on aid that were wiped out."[1] Israel targeted critical civilian infrastructure, such as the only operative flour mill and nearly all of the cement factories, so that Gaza would be ever more dependent on Israeli whim for staples and would not be able to rebuild after a cease-fire went into effect.[2]

A year and a half after Cast Lead, major humanitarian and human rights organizations uniformly attested that the people of Gaza continued to suffer a humanitarian crisis on account of the Israeli siege: "Contrary to what the Israeli government states, the humanitarian aid allowed into Gaza is only a fraction of what is needed to answer the enormous needs of an exhausted people" (Oxfam); "The blockade ... has severely damaged the economy, leaving 70 to 80 percent of Gazans in poverty" (Human Rights Watch); "Israel is blocking vital medical supplies from entering the Gaza Strip" (World Health Organization); "The closure is having a devastating impact on the 1.5 million people living in Gaza" (International Committee of the Red Cross).[3]

On 31 May 2010, a humanitarian flotilla en route to Gaza carrying some 10,000 tons of supplies and 700 passengers came under attack in international waters by Israeli commandos. By the end of the night-time Israeli assault, nine passengers aboard the flagship *Mavi Marmara* had been shot dead. Eight were Turkish citizens, one was a dual US-Turkish citizen. The details of the massacre are in an important respect beside the point. The consensus among human rights and humanitarian organizations was and remains that the Israeli blockade of Gaza constitutes a form of collective punishment in flagrant violation of international law. Israel accordingly had no right to use force to enforce an illegal blockade.[4] Israel's concomitant claim that its attack on the *Mavi Marmara* was an act of self-defense also does not pass legal muster. A tenet of law establishes that no legal benefit or right can be derived from an illegal act (*ex injuria non oritur jus*). Consequently, Israel cannot claim a right of self-defense that arises because of its illegal blockade. On the other hand, the passengers aboard a convoy in international waters carrying humanitarian relief to a beleaguered population had every right to use force in self-defense against what was, in effect, a pirate raid.[5]

Still, it bears notice that Israel's explanation for the deaths has been refuted by authoritative accounts of what transpired. The official Israeli account would have it that peaceful commandos armed only with "paintball rifles" were "ambushed" and "lynched" by a phalanx of "radical anti-Western," "machete-wielding," "bloodthirsty" "*jihadists*," and that the Israelis used armed force only "as a last resort" in "self-defense."[6] In fact, Israeli combatants in inflatable boats abutting the *Mavi Marmara* opened fire with tear gas, smoke and stun grenades, and perhaps plastic bullets, and helicopters hovering above then opened fire with live ammunition before any commando had rappelled on deck;[7] the passengers—none of whom were linked with a terrorist organization at the time of the attack[8]—did not even prepare for injuries[9] and neither possessed firearms nor discharged ones they seized;[10] captured Israeli commandos were given medical care and then escorted for release;[11] and, far from firing with restraint and only in self-defense, the Israeli commandos killed the nine passengers by shooting all but one of them multiple times—five were shot in the head, and at least six were killed in a manner consistent with an extra-legal, arbitrary and summary execution.[12]

Even if, for argument's sake, one credits Israel's right to block passage of a humanitarian flotilla, its account still makes little sense. The question remains, "why, on a supposedly peaceful interception, its commandos chose to board the ship by rappelling from a military helicopter, in the dark, in international waters," in a fashion practically designed to induce panic.[13] Israel could have chosen—as Israeli officials readily acknowledged—from an array of relatively benign options, such as disabling the propeller, rudder or engine of the vessel and towing it to the Israeli port at Ashdod, or physically blocking the vessel's passage.[14] Furthermore, a quasi-official

Israeli report issued after the commando raid repeatedly emphasized that "throughout the planning process" Israeli authorities at all levels anticipated that "the participants in the flotilla were all peaceful civilians" and "seem not to have believed that the use of force would be necessary." They had "expected" the commandos to meet "at most, verbal resistance, pushing or punching," "relatively minor civil disobedience," "some pushing and limited physical contact." The Israeli report quoted the commandos themselves testifying that "we were expected to encounter activists who would try to hurt us emotionally by creating provocations on the level of curses, spitting . . . but we did not expect a difficult physical confrontation"; "we were expected to encounter peace activists and therefore the prospect that we would have to use weapons or other means was . . . nearly zero probability."[15] But if it didn't expect forceful resistance, why didn't Israel launch the operation in broad daylight, indeed, bringing in tow a complement of journalists who could vouch for its nonviolent intentions? An operation launched in the blackness of night would appear to make sense only if Israel wanted to sow confusion as a prelude to a violent assault, and in order to obscure from potential witnesses its methods of attack. But to what end? In fact, multiple factors converged to make a violent commando raid Israel's preferred modus operandi.

In recent years, Israel has conducted a succession of bungled security operations. In 2006, it suffered a major military setback in Lebanon. It tried restoring its deterrence capacity—i.e., the Arab-Muslim world's fear of it—during Cast Lead. However, the assault evoked not awe at Israel's martial prowess but disgust at its lethal cowardice. Then, in early 2010, Israel dispatched a commando team to assassinate a Hamas leader in Dubai but, although the mission was accomplished, the unit ended up seeding a diplomatic storm on account of its amateurish execution. Israel was now desperate to restore its derring-do image of bygone years. What better way than an Entebbe-like commando raid?[16]

Among the vessels comprising the humanitarian flotilla, the resort to violent force was most egregious in the assault on the *Mavi Marmara*. Some two-thirds of the 600 passengers on this vessel were Turkish citizens, while the core contingent was alleged to be "a front for a radical Islamist organization, probably with links to the ruling party in Turkey," making the *Mavi Marmara* a yet more tempting target.[17] Recall that Turkish Prime Minister Recep Tayyip Erdoğan has become increasingly outspoken in his criticism of Israel and in his determination to carve out an independent foreign policy. The flotilla represented, for Israel, a unique opportunity to cut the Turkish upstart down to size; a sleek (if bloody) commando raid would remind Ankara who was in charge.

The use of violent force was also Israel's response of last resort to stem the increasing number of vessels destined for Gaza. It initially allowed shipborne humanitarian supplies to pass through, no doubt hoping that the spirits of the organizers would eventually peter out as public interest flagged. When this didn't happen, the Israeli navy rammed and intercepted vessels en route to Gaza.[18] But the ships kept coming. Is it so surprising that Israel would then turn to violent force? After Israel prevented a humanitarian ship from reaching Gaza in early 2009, a British-led delegation "worried" out loud to US embassy officials in Beirut "that the Israeli government would not be as 'lenient' in the future should similar incidents occur."[19] If the assault on the flotilla couldn't have shocked those in the loop, it also didn't shock seasoned observers of the Israeli scene. The "violent interception of civilian vessels carrying humanitarian aid," Israeli novelist Amos Oz reflected, was the "rank product" of the Israeli "mantra that what can't be done by force can be done with even greater force."[20]

As it happened, Israel's assault on the *Mavi Marmara* turned into yet another botched operation. The once vaunted Israel Defense Forces (IDF) has become, as political scientist John J. Mearsheimer put it, "the gang that cannot shoot straight."[21] It is hard to exaggerate the cost—at any rate, in Israeli eyes—of this latest misadventure. Although Israeli *hasbara* desperately sought to spin the raid as an "operational success"[22] and the commandos as untarnished heroes, few were taken in. Israeli pundits deplored the "disgraceful fiasco" and "national humiliation," in which "deterrence took a bad blow."[23] "The magic evaporated long ago, the most moral army in the world, that was once the best army in the world, failed again," Gideon Levy half mocked. "More and more there is the impression that nearly everything it touches causes harm to Israel."[24]

The Naval Commandos comprise Israel's "best fighting unit";[25] they had rehearsed the attack for weeks, even constructing a model of the *Mavi Marmara*.[26] Nonetheless, when 30 of these commandos faced off against an equal number of civilian passengers possessing only makeshift weapons, three of them not only allowed themselves to be captured, but photographs of them being *nursed* went viral on the Web. Israeli soldiers—and commandos above all—are not supposed to be taken alive, especially after the capture in 2006 of Israeli soldier Gilad Shalit turned into a national trauma.[27] One widely quoted *Mavi Marmara* passenger who disarmed the commandos recalled afterwards, "They looked like frightened children in the face of an abusive father."[28]

A cohort of "frightened children" is not the image Israel wants to project to foe or friend of its fighting force. "The claim made by the IDF spokesman that the soldiers' lives were in danger and they feared a lynching," a *Haaretz* military analyst understatedly opined, "is hardly complimentary to the men of the elite naval units."[29] The image also cannot give much comfort to Israel's own population. Will it, after so many military misadventures, grow jittery of the IDF's ability to subdue a seemingly endless list of ever more potent enemies? "It's one thing for people to think you're crazy," an Israeli general rued, "but it's bad when they think you're incompetent and crazy, and that's the way we look."[30] The results of a 2010 poll in the Arab world showing that only 12 percent of the Arab public believed Israel was "very powerful" while fully 44 percent believed it was "weaker than it looks" validated, and probably exacerbated, the anxieties of Israelis.[31] Each disastrous mission ups the stakes. At some point, Israel must launch a yet more spectacular (and lethal) operation to compensate for its long string of military failures. The only question is, not *if*, but *when* and *where*.[32]

Despite the irretrievable loss of human life—indeed, *because* of it—the historic achievement of the Freedom Flotilla should not be lost from sight. A nonviolent, international grassroots initiative proved able to force the hands of the world's mightiest states. In an abrupt volte-face on the morning after the flotilla bloodbath, Western leaders, such as US Secretary of State Hillary Clinton and British Foreign Secretary William Hague, discovered individually, and the United Nations Security Council discovered collectively, that Israel's siege of Gaza was "unsustainable" and had to be lifted.[33] In fact, Israeli

Prime Minister Benjamin Netanyahu himself had to concede the existence of the Israeli siege and the necessity of terminating it.[34] The prison gates of Gaza have so far been pried open only a few inches at most,[35] but those inches manifest the latent power of a mass nonviolent movement built on the simple truth that the siege is inhuman and unjust.

True, the international community would probably not have pressured Israel were it not for the Turkish state's high decibel intervention. The grassroots movement in and of itself, and however many its mortal sacrifices, is not yet able to inflect state policy. On its own, the murder of Rachel Corrie did not rattle American complicity with the Israeli occupation, nor did the murder of Tom Hurndall rattle British complicity. Nor has the heroic nonviolent resistance in West Bank villages like Bil'in yet stirred the world's conscience. But the solidarity movement is still in a nascent stage and has yet to draw on its vast reserves. One can only imagine the potential of a movement that taps the dormant talent and ingenuity of its ever-expanding ranks; of a committed leadership that harnesses this restless but diffuse energy and doesn't let petty jealousies, turf wars and ego aggrandizement obscure the common objective; of one, two, three, many flotillas determined to break the cruel siege, once and for all. Energizing as these prospects might be, one must simultaneously bear in mind the magnitude of the will that is required, how concentrated, tenacious and sustained this collective will needs to be, in order to extract even the most meager concession from those ruthlessly wielding power. Despite the universal condemnation of Israel's commando raid, and the concerted calls by world leaders for Israel to lift the siege of Gaza, there was still "no tangible change for the people on the ground"[36] in the ensuing months, while the humanitarian crisis again vanished from the headlines.

The fact that the murders of Corrie and Hurndall still resonate and that the murder of nine foreigners aboard the *Mavi Marmara* evoked global condemnation should serve as a fillip to the solidarity movement. However unfair, it remains true that a higher value is attached to some lives—and deaths—than others; that Palestinian lives are expendable, while the lives of foreigners are not. The US Civil Rights Movement immortalized the names Schwerner and Goodman, and who can deny the nobility of their sacrifice? Yet, a forgotten Black person was killed in Mississippi in each of the five months preceding the deaths of these two white (and Jewish) volunteers in Freedom Summer.[37] The inequality in valuating life should outrage, but it should also prod us to redouble our commitment because the presence of a "higher-graded" life can direct attention to an atrocity that would otherwise go unnoticed.

A skeptic might wonder whether the bloody spectacle aboard the *Mavi Marmara* proved the power of nonviolence or, in fact, of violence. Would the world have paid heed if the passengers had not forcefully resisted and the Israeli killings had not ensued? But such a reading of what happened doubly errs. At some point, Israel's resort to massive bloodshed was inevitable, however peaceful the opposition. The death toll on the *Mavi Marmara* was probably greater than Israel intended, but ultimately Israel has no recourse except to lethal force against determined nonviolent resistance. Moreover, nonviolent resistance does not preclude but, in fact, is predicated on the prospect of mortal self-sacrifice. Mahatma Gandhi *demanded* of *satyagrahis* that they seek out martyrdom at the hands of their oppressors: for, the whole point of nonviolent resistance was to prick the public conscience into action against injustice.[38] No sight was more likely to arouse respect than innocents willing to die for their basic rights, and no sight was more likely to arouse indignation than innocents being killed for aspiring to these rights; indeed, the willingness to die nonviolently in pursuit of these rights affirmed the victims' worthiness of them. Although it appalled grassroots activists, some leaders of the Civil Rights Movement were "elated" when Southern segregationists sicked dogs on nonviolent demonstrators. "They said over and over again," James Foreman bitterly recounted, "'We've got a movement. We've got a movement. They brought out the dogs. We've got a movement!'"[39] The promise of nonviolence is not that it will preempt suffering and death but, as Gandhi never tired of repeating, that it can achieve the same results as violence at far lesser cost. Or, as a Hamas legislator put it, "The Gaza flotilla has done more for Gaza than 10,000 rockets."[40]

The overarching lesson of the *Mavi Marmara* is to focus, not up above on meaningless sideshows like the "peace process," but on summoning forth our own internal capacities. Instead of hoping against hope that President Barack Obama will yet redeem himself, our challenge is to muster sufficient political will from below so that he does the right thing—or, at any rate, doesn't keep doing the wrong thing—*regardless* of what he wants. Deferring to the powers on high or waiting for a messiah is a confession of impotence. The simple but fundamental truth of politics, which even the most resolute of atheists would hasten to affirm, is that God helps those who help themselves.

Although the *Mavi Marmara* bloodbath marked yet another data point in the decline of Israel's global standing,[41] still, public opinion has yet to be organized into an effective political force, and Israel was able to contain the immediate diplomatic and legal fallout.

In a gesture designed to placate Turkey, UN Secretary-General Ban Ki-moon appointed on 2 August 2010 a Panel of Inquiry (hereafter: UN Panel) to "examine and identify the facts, circumstances and context of the incident," and to "consider and recommend ways of avoiding similar incidents in the future."[42] Israel initially opposed an international investigation but then reversed itself, proclaiming it had "nothing to hide,"[43] after Ban Ki-moon eviscerated the proposed panel's mandate[44] and appointed as its vice-chair the singularly corrupt and criminal Colombian ex-president Alvaro Uribe, who is also an outspoken proponent of closer military ties between Colombia and Israel.[45] It was predictable—and predicted at the time—that the panel would produce a whitewash.[46] In the event, the report it produced, which vindicated Israel's claim that its naval blockade of Gaza is legal, is probably the most mendacious and debased document ever issued under the aegis of the United Nations.

The UN Panel alleges that, in light of the "real threat" posed by Hamas rocket and mortar attacks, Israel's naval blockade of Gaza constituted a "legitimate security measure" and "complied with the requirements of international law."[47] Its conclusions flatly contradicted those reached by other authorities, which unanimously judged Israel's blockade a "flagrant violation of international law" (Amnesty International).[48] Waving aside the findings of human rights organizations came easily to vice-chair Uribe who, in one of his periodic rants against these organizations, had earlier denounced Amnesty's "blindness" and "fanaticism."[49]

The argument contrived by the UN Panel to justify Israel's naval blockade consists of a sequence of interrelated propositions:

1. The Israeli naval blockade of Gaza was unrelated to the Israeli land blockade;
2. Israel confronted a significant security threat from Gaza's coastal waters;
3. Israel imposed the naval blockade in response to this security threat;
4. The naval blockade was the only means Israel had at its disposal to meet the threat posed by the flotillas;
5. The Israeli naval blockade achieved its security objective without causing disproportionate harm to Gaza's civilian population.

To pronounce the naval blockade legal, the UN Panel had to sustain each and every one of these propositions. If even one were false, its defense of the blockade collapsed. The astonishing thing is that they are *all* false. Each will be addressed in turn.

THE ISRAELI NAVAL BLOCKADE OF GAZA WAS UNRELATED TO THE ISRAELI LAND BLOCKADE. The critical first premise of the UN Panel is that the Israeli naval blockade was both conceptually and practically "distinct from" the land blockade.[50] In fact, however, in design as well as implementation, the Israeli land and naval blockades constituted complementary halves of a unified whole: both served identical functions, while the success of each was essential to the success of the other. The Israeli government itself acknowledged these points.

Since the inception of its occupation in 1967, Israel has regulated passage of goods and persons along Gaza's land and coastal borders. After Hamas gained full control of Gaza in 2007, Israel imposed a yet more stringent blockade on it.[51] The blockade was conceived to perform a twofold function: (a) a *security* objective of preventing weapons from reaching Gaza, and (b) a *political* objective of "bringing Gaza's economy to the brink of collapse"—as Israeli officials repeatedly put it in private—in order to punish Gazans for electing Hamas and to turn them against it. The list of items Israel barred from entering Gaza—such as chocolate, chips, and baby chicks—pointed up the irreducibly *political* dimension of the blockade.[52]

Even the Turkel Commission, a quasi-official Israeli inquiry that unsurprisingly vindicated Israel on all key points regarding the flotilla assault,[53] did not contest the dual security-political purpose of the naval blockade. For example, its final report cited testimony by Tzipi Livni, who was Israel's foreign minister when the naval blockade was imposed, as well as a document delineating the purposes behind the blockade submitted by Major-General (res.) Amos Gilad, head of the Political, Military and Policy Affairs Bureau at Israel's Ministry of Defense:

> Tzipi Livni said . . . that the imposition of the naval blockade . . . was done in a wider context, as part of Israel's comprehensive strategy (which she referred to as a "dual strategy") of delegitimizing Hamas on the one hand and strengthening the status of the Palestinian Authority vis-à-vis the Gaza Strip on the other. . . . According to her approach, . . . the attempts to transfer [humanitarian] goods to the Gaza Strip by sea . . . give legitimacy to the Hamas regime in the Gaza Strip. . . . Livni also stated that *it would be a mistake*

to examine the circumstances of imposing the naval
blockade from a narrow security perspective only.
. . .

The document [by Gilad] contains two considerations [regarding the blockade]: one . . . is to
prevent any military strengthening of the Hamas;
the other . . . is to "isolate and weaken Hamas." In
this context, Major-General (res.) Gilad stated that
the significance of opening a maritime route to
the Gaza Strip was that the Hamas's status would
be strengthened significantly from economic and
political viewpoints. He further stated that opening a maritime route to the Gaza Strip, particu-
larly while it is under Hamas control, . . . would
be tantamount of [sic] a "very significant achievement for Hamas." . . . Major-General (res.) Gilad
concluded: "In summary, the need to impose
a naval blockade on the Gaza Strip arises from
security and military considerations . . . and also
to prevent any legitimization and economic and
political strengthening of Hamas and strengthening
it in the internal Palestinian arena [vis-à-vis the
Palestinian Authority in the West Bank]."

"It would therefore appear," the Commission concluded, "that even though the purpose of the naval blockade was fundamentally a security one in response to military needs, *its imposition was also regarded by the decision makers as legitimate within the concept of Israel's comprehensive 'dual strategy' against the Hamas in the Gaza Strip.*"[54]

The Israeli Turkel Report also did not contest that the naval blockade was *integral* to the strategy of achieving the twin goals. Indeed, it explicitly maintained that the land and sea blockade must be treated as a seamless whole:

> Both the naval blockade and the land crossings policy were imposed and implemented because of the prolonged international armed conflict between Israel and the Hamas. . . . [O]n the strategic level . . . the naval blockade is regarded by the Government as part of Israel's wider effort not to give legitimacy to the Hamas's rule over the Gaza Strip, to isolate it in the international arena, and to strengthen the Palestinian Authority.

The report further pointed out that "the naval blockade is also connected to the land crossings policy on a tactical level": if and when cargo aboard vessels headed for Gaza was rerouted through the land crossings, it was subject to the land restrictions blocking passage of critical goods, such as "iron and cement."[55] "Therefore," the report concluded, "it is possible that the enforcement of the naval blockade in addition to the implementation of the land crossings policy has a humanitarian impact on the population, at least in principle"; *"The approach of the Israeli Government . . . created, in this sense, a connection regarding the humanitarian effect on the Gaza Strip between the naval blockade and the land crossings policy."*[56]

Because the Israeli Turkel Report held that the land and naval blockades were "in principle" inextricably intertwined, it could defend the legality of the Israeli naval blockade only by simultaneously upholding the propriety of the land blockade and treating each "in conjunction"[57] with the other. The UN Panel was consequently confronted with a dilemma. If it retraced the Israeli Turkel Report's line of argumentation, it would have to pass judgment on Israel's blockade policy as a whole. But if it rendered such a comprehensive judgment, the UN Panel could vindicate Israel only by blatantly contradicting the near-unanimous authoritative opinion that declared such a blockade illegal.[58] The UN Panel accordingly resolved on an altogether novel strategy. It artificially pried the land blockade from the naval blockade, relegated the land blockade to a secondary and side issue, and proceeded to focus in its legal analysis exclusively on the naval blockade as if it were a thing apart.[59]

To justify this radical surgical procedure, the UN Panel points to the facts that, chronologically, imposition of the land blockade (in 2007) preceded imposition of the naval blockade (in 2009); that the "intensity" of the land blockade "fluctuated" over time whereas the naval blockade "has not been altered since its imposition"; and that the naval blockade "was imposed primarily to enable . . . Israel to exert control over ships attempting to reach Gaza with weapons and related goods."[60] This series of affirmations confuses and conflates the broad purposes behind Israel's blockade policy with the practical modalities of its enforcement. Since 2007, Israel has imposed a suffocating blockade on all of Gaza's borders. This comprehensive blockade has been designed to achieve the dual goals of preventing weapons from reaching Gaza and politically isolating Hamas. Although

Israel periodically adjusted its blockade policies to accommodate new political contingencies, the dual security-political goals stayed constant. It is disingenuous to pretend that, as against the security *and* political dimensions of the Israeli land blockade, the purpose of the coastal blockade was "primarily"—in fact, in its legal analysis the UN Panel effectively argues that it was *exclusively*—to prevent weapons from reaching Gaza. The ultimate irony is that, *senso stricto*, the naval blockade did serve only one of the two purposes, but it was *not* the military one; its purpose was narrowly political. The UN Panel is thus doubly wrong: the naval blockade was not "distinct from" the land blockade, and the purpose of the naval blockade was not "primarily" security.

ISRAEL CONFRONTED A SIGNIFICANT SECURITY THREAT FROM GAZA'S COASTAL WATERS. "The fundamental principle of the freedom of navigation on the high seas," the UN Panel observes, "is subject to only certain limited exceptions under international law."[61] A State party attempting to restrict navigation hence bears a heavy legal burden. It inexorably flows from these tenets that the greater the impediment a state places on freedom of navigation, the heavier its legal burden. If a fundamental freedom is at stake, then infringements on it must be graduated: an extreme restriction would not be justified if a lesser restriction would meet the perceived threat. In the case at hand, if the "visit and search" of a vessel (where there are "reasonable grounds" for suspicion) is an effective means of preventing contraband[62] from reaching Gaza, then it cannot be justified to impose the more restrictive measure of a naval blockade that, by indiscriminately barring passage of all goods, military and nonmilitary, obstructs commercial traffic and potentially inflicts grave harm on the civilian population.[63]

The UN Panel purports that Israel confronted a significant security threat from Gaza's coastal waters that could be met only by a naval blockade. However, the evidence it brings to bear in support of this contention underwhelms. It cites, on the basis of the Israeli Turkel Report, *three* alleged instances of attempted weapons smuggling into Gaza by sea, the last of which, in 2003, had occurred *six years before* Israel's imposition of the naval blockade.[64] It further alleges, citing the Turkel Report, that after its 2005 "disengagement," Israel had to find a new legal basis for preventing weapons from reaching Gaza. Even if true, it still would not explain why the visit and search method apparently proved effective after the 2005 "disengagement" until some-time in mid-2008, when it abruptly presented what the UN Panel, following the Turkel Report, calls "practical difficulties."[65] The UN Panel, citing the Turkel Report, also alleges that only a naval blockade provided a legal basis for preventing Hamas from smuggling weapons out of Gaza to launch attacks from the sea.[66] But it cites no instances—none apparently exists—of Hamas attempting such a maneuver.

ISRAEL IMPOSED THE NAVAL BLOCKADE IN RESPONSE TO THIS SECURITY THREAT. The UN Panel alleges, on the basis of the Israeli Turkel Report, that Israel imposed the naval blockade "in order to prevent weapons, terrorists and money from entering or exiting the Gaza Strip by sea."[67] But, although Israel formally gestured to this threat as its rationale for imposing the naval block-ade, the UN Panel does not present a persuasive case for crediting this official Israeli testimony. In its legal analysis of the naval blockade, the UN Panel's method-ology amounts to, *If Israel says so, it must be true.*[68]

In fact, Israel imposed the naval blockade not because it faced a security threat from the sea but, on the contrary, because it did *not* face one. As the Israeli Turkel Report observed, Israel couldn't rely on visit and search to block flotillas from Gaza, because those powers can be used only against vessels suspected of carrying weapons. Israel's quandary was that the Gaza flotillas did not carry weapons and that it therefore lacked a legal basis for stopping them. Israel initially let a succession of vessels pass, *not even bothering to search them*, in the hope that the flotilla phenomenon would go away.[69] When the ships kept coming, Israel responded with escalating violence—but still they kept coming. It was "in these circumstances, on January 3, 2009," the Turkel Report recalled, that "the Minister of Defense ordered a naval blockade. . . . The significance of imposing a naval blockade according to the rules of international law is that it allows a party to an armed conflict to prevent entry into the prohibited area of any vessel that attempts to breach the blockade (*even without it being established that the vessel is assisting terrorist activity*)."[70] That is, the blockade was imposed in order to provide Israel with a legal basis for preventing passage of vessels transporting not weapons but humanitarian cargo to Gaza.

THE NAVAL BLOCKADE WAS THE ONLY MEANS ISRAEL HAD AT ITS DISPOSAL TO MEET THE THREAT POSED BY THE FLOTILLAS. Even if, for argument's sake, the claim were credited that, as a practical matter and setting aside the law, no country at war would permit a convoy of ships—even a declared humanitarian convoy that had been carefully searched—to pass freely into enemy territory, Israel still had another ready option. The UN Panel itself alludes, if only in passing and in another context, to this alternative. It reports that "at a briefing immediately after the 31 May 2010 incident, a senior United Nations official noted that the loss of life could have been avoided if Israel had responded to repeated calls to end its closure of Gaza."[71] Thus, if Israel wanted to stop the humanitarian convoys headed for Gaza, all it needed do was lift the illegal economic blockade that was causing a humanitarian crisis. Revealingly, this obvious option did not figure in the UN Panel's analysis of the naval blockade's legality. Was it because, in the face of this option, Israel's only conceivable justification for the naval blockade crumbled and, consequently, the UN Panel could vindicate Israel only by defending the patently indefensible policy of a comprehensive siege that amounted to collective punishment?

THE ISRAELI NAVAL BLOCKADE ACHIEVED ITS SECURITY OBJECTIVE WITHOUT CAUSING DISPROPORTIONATE HARM TO GAZA'S CIVILIAN POPULATION. The UN Panel contends that, given the "absence of significant port facilities in Gaza," the harm caused by the naval blockade to Gaza's civilian population was "slight," and therefore—according to the proportionality test of international humanitarian law— not disproportionate to the military gain.[72] But if, as the evidence unambiguously shows, the Israeli naval block- ade did not serve the purpose of self-defense but instead was imposed with a political objective in mind, then the proportionality test is wholly irrelevant. As the UN Panel observes, "The imposition of a blockade must have a lawful military objective."[73] Put otherwise, even if the humanitarian value of the maritime point of entry were limited, the naval blockade would still cause proportion- ally greater harm because its military value was nil—or, at any rate, whatever military objective it met could also have been met by a visit and search procedure that did not hinder the passage of humanitarian goods.

Furthermore, even if the naval blockade did serve a military objective, it would still be hasty to conclude that it did not cause disproportionate collateral damage.

The Israeli Turkel Report itself cautioned against being too dismissive of Gaza's potential for maritime traffic: if goods could just barely enter Gaza by sea, then it must follow that weapons, too, could just barely enter—which in turn would render a naval blockade redundant and any justification for it unsustainable.[74] The furthest the Turkel Report would go was, "in the absence of information and records, it is difficult to determine the effect of the naval blockade alone on the humanitarian situation in the Gaza Strip."[75] It cannot but perplex how the UN Panel knew the potential harm of the naval blockade was "slight" when even the egregiously apologetic Israeli Turkel Report pleaded agnosticism.

Once having proven that the Israeli naval blockade was legal, the UN Panel proceeds to reprimand the flotilla passengers for having committed a "dangerous and reckless act" by attempting to breach it.[76] The UN Panel also repeatedly exhorts states to proactively prevent such irresponsible undertakings in the future.[77] The welfare of Gaza and its people, the UN Panel suggests, would be better served by and should be the exclusive preserve of states, not ordinary citizens. Consider what would have transpired had this advice been heeded.

In 2007, Israel imposed a stringent blockade on Gaza that constituted a form of collective punishment and consequently a flagrant violation of international law. The international community did not lift a finger. Journeying to Gaza around this time, former High Commissioner for Human Rights Mary Robinson declared that Gaza's "whole civilization has been destroyed, I'm not exaggerating." The international community still did not lift a finger. In November 2008, Israel turned the blockade's screws yet tighter, bringing Gaza's infrastructure "to the brink of collapse." The international community still did not lift a finger. "The breakdown of an entire society is happening in front of us," Harvard political economist Sara Roy wrote in the *London Review of Books*, "but there is little international response."[78]

In late December 2008, Israel launched Operation Cast Lead and, in the course of what Amnesty called "22 days of death and destruction," it massacred the Gazan civilian population and laid waste the civilian infrastructure. In January 2009, the UN Security Council finally reacted to popular international outrage at Israel's crimes by passing a resolution (1860) that expressed "grave concern . . . at the deepening humanitarian crisis in Gaza," and called for "the unimpeded provision and distribution throughout Gaza of humanitarian assistance, including of food, fuel and medical treatment." Israel nonetheless persisted in its strangulating blockade, and the international community still did not lift a finger. It was only *after* the martyrdom of the *Mavi Marmara* passengers, as the UN Panel itself effectively concedes,[79] that the world's leaders suddenly awakened to the realization that the Israeli blockade was "unsustainable," and some (albeit grossly insufficient) relief was granted to Gaza's desperate civilian population. But if the UN Panel had had its way, and the Freedom Flotilla had not taken the initiative to commit a "dangerous and reckless act" that—God forbid!—infringed on the sacred prerogatives of states, Israel would have been left undisturbed and the people of Gaza left to languish and expire.

Although the UN Panel deemed Israel's killing of the nine passengers "unacceptable,"[80] it strove hard to "balance" this assessment by also casting doubt on the passengers' character. Here again it confronted a dilemma.

The Israeli Turkel Report alleged that the organizers of the flagship *Mavi Marmara* were *jihadis* hell-bent on killing Israelis. It had some difficulty sustaining this charge, however, because the most lethal weapons "smuggled" on board by these would-be *jihadis*, according to the Turkel Report itself, were slingshots and glass marbles, while it was hard to explain why these young, burly fanatics did not manage to kill a single Israeli commando, not even the three who were being held captive by them.[81]

Just as the UN Panel adopted a novel strategy to prove the legality of the blockade, so it also conjured a creative proof that the Israeli Turkel Report's condemnation of these alleged *jihadis* was on the mark. The UN Panel "seriously questions the true nature and objectives of the flotilla organizers." Why? Because it discovered that they intended not only to deliver humanitarian relief, but also "to generate publicity about the situation in Gaza." To clinch its indictment, the UN Panel reproduces with a great flourish this incriminating document "prepared by" the organizers:

> Purpose: Purposes of this journey are to create an awareness amongst world public and international

organizations on the inhumane and unjust embargo on Palestine and to contribute to end this embargo which clearly violates human rights and delivering humanitarian relief to the Palestinians.[82]

The UN Panel goes on to adduce yet more evidence of this sinister and nefarious plot: "The number of journalists embarked on the ships gives further power to the conclusion that the flotilla's primary purpose was to generate publicity."[83] Not even the wretched Israeli Turkel Report dared impugn the passengers' motive of publicizing the blockade's dire impact.[84] It must be a first, and surely marks a nadir, in the annals of the United Nations that a report bearing its imprimatur vilifies the victims of a murderous assault because they sought to cast light on a crime against humanity.[85]

5/ GO AHEAD, INVADE! (2012)

ON 14 NOVEMBER 2012, Israel launched Operation Pillar of Defense. According to the official story line, the assault began only after it had stoically absorbed hundreds of Hamas projectile attacks. The facts, however, suggest otherwise. From the start of 2012, one Israeli had been killed as a result of Palestinian attacks from Gaza, whereas 78 Palestinians had been killed by Israeli strikes. Hamas had mostly steered clear of armed confrontations. In the methodical madness that is Israeli policy towards Gaza, Ahmed al-Jaabari, the Hamas leader whose assassination by Israel triggered the new round of fighting, had served as Israel's "subcontractor" for enforcing the periodic cease-fires;[1] in fact, he was in the process of "advancing a permanent cease-fire agreement" when Israel liquidated him.[2] But Hamas also recoiled at the prospect of becoming a clone of the collaborationist Palestinian Authority (PA). It occasionally turned a blind eye, or joined in (if only to prevent an escalation), when Israeli provocations resulted in retaliatory strikes by Hamas's more militant Islamist rivals.

At the time Israel launched Pillar of Defense, it was widely speculated that Hamas had been itching for a fight. On every front, however, Hamas had been on a roll prior to the outbreak of hostilities. Its ideological soul mate, the Muslim Brotherhood, had risen to power in Egypt. The emir of Qatar had journeyed to Gaza carrying the promise of $400 million in aid, while Turkish Prime Minister Recep Tayyip Erdoğan was scheduled to arrive shortly. In the West Bank, many Palestinians envied Gaza's (imagined) economic prosperity. In the meantime, Gaza's Islamic University had even managed to pull off an academic conference attended by renowned linguist Noam Chomsky. Hamas's star was slowly but surely rising, at the expense of the hapless PA. The very last thing it needed at that juncture was an inevitably destructive confrontation with Israel that could jeopardize these hard-won, steadily accreting gains.

On the other side, some cynical Israelis speculated that Prime Minister Benjamin Netanyahu launched Pillar of Defense to boost his chances in the upcoming election.

As a general rule, however, Israeli leaders would not undertake major military operations or jeopardize critical state interests for the sake of partisan electoral gain. It was also purported that Israel's governing coalition had to do something to appease popular indignation at the Hamas projectiles. But in fact, they had barely registered on Israel's political radar; public opinion was focused on the Islamic Republic of Iran and sundry domestic issues.

Why, then, did Israel attack?

In one sense, Israel was transparent about its motive. It kept repeating that it wanted to restore its "deterrence capacity." The real puzzle is the nature of the threat it sought to deter. Pillar of Defense unfolded in the broader context of successive Israeli foreign policy failures. Netanyahu had endeavored to rally the international community for an attack on Iran, but ended up looking the fool as he held up in the United Nations a comic-strip depiction of The Iranian Bomb. Hezbollah boasted that a drone launched by it had penetrated Israeli airspace, and reserved the right to enter Israeli airspace at its whim. Now, the Party of God's "terrorist" twin upstart in Gaza was gaining respectability as regional powers thumbed their collective nose at Israel on its doorstep. The natives were getting restless. It was time to take out the big club and crack a few skulls to remind the locals who was in charge—or, in Israel's preferred metaphor, it was time to "mow the grass" again in Gaza. "At the heart of Operation Pillar of Defense," the Crisis Group observed, "lay an effort to demonstrate that Hamas's newfound confidence was altogether premature and that, the Islamist awakening notwithstanding, changes in the Middle East would not change much at all."[3]

Still, Israel needed a credible alibi. In November 2008, it had broken the cease-fire (by killing six Hamas militants) in order to provoke a retaliatory attack by Hamas, which then supplied the pretext for Operation Cast Lead. Four years later, it killed Jaabari to provoke Hamas again and supply the pretext for Pillar of Defense. The actual Israeli assault, however, differed significantly from Cast Lead. It was qualitatively less murderous and destructive. Israel, it was said, used more precise weapons during Pillar of Defense and had "learned the lessons" of Cast Lead on how to avoid civilian casualties. In fact, 99 percent of Israeli air strikes during Cast Lead hit targets accurately, while its manifest goal was—in the words of the Goldstone Report, which was corroborated by scores of other human rights reports—to "punish, humiliate and terrorize" the Gazan civilian population.[4]

If its new rampage proved less lethal by comparison, it was not because Israel had corrected for past errors, but because of the unprecedented political constraints to which it was subject. *First*, Turkey and Egypt had made abundantly clear that they would not sit idly by if Israel launched a repeat performance of Cast Lead. From early on, both states drew a red line at an Israeli ground assault. Although officially denied now,[5] it was reliably reported at the time that President Barack Obama, no doubt prodded by these key regional actors, counseled Israel not to invade. *Second*, the prospect of another Goldstone Report hung over Israel. After Cast Lead, Israeli officials had managed to elude prosecution at the International Criminal Court as well as legal accountability elsewhere (on the basis of universal jurisdiction). But, if it committed another massacre, Israel might not again be so fortunate. *Third*, Gaza was swarming with foreign journalists. Israel had sealed Gaza shut from the outside world before Cast Lead with the collaboration of Hosni Mubarak's Egypt. In the initial phase of that onslaught, Israel had enjoyed a near-total monopoly on media coverage. But this time around, journalists could freely enter Gaza and incontrovertibly report Israeli atrocities in real time. On account of this trio of factors, during Pillar of Defense Israel mostly targeted sites that could be deemed "legitimate." True, some 70 Palestinian civilians were killed, but that could be chalked up to "collateral damage."

The deaths and injuries of civilians during Pillar of Defense, although far fewer than in previous rounds of the conflict, received in-depth and graphic news coverage. When Israel tested the limits of military legitimacy, trouble loomed. After it flattened civilian governmental structures in Gaza, the headline on the *New York Times* website read, "Israel targets civilian buildings." A few hours later it metamorphosed into "*government* buildings" (no doubt after a call from the Israeli consulate). Still, the writing was on the wall: Israeli conduct was being closely scrutinized by outsiders, so it had better tread carefully. The egregious exceptions came during the cease-fire negotiations when Israel resorted to its standard precision terror tactics in order to extract the best possible terms in a final agreement, and also targeted journalists in the event that negotiations collapsed and it would have to, after all, launch a murderous ground invasion.

The armed resistance Hamas put up during the eight-day Israeli assault was largely symbolic. Although Israel reveled in the success of its newly deployed Iron Dome antimissile defense system,[6] it almost certainly did not save many, and perhaps not any, lives. During Cast Lead some 925 "rockets" (and an additional number of mortar shells) landing in Israel killed three Israeli civilians, while during Pillar of Defense some 850 "rockets" (and an additional number of mortar shells) landing in Israel killed four Israeli civilians. It is unlikely that, in the main and allowing for the aberration, Hamas used more sophisticated weapons during Pillar of Defense. Through its army of informers and its state-of-the-art aerial surveillance, Israel would have been privy to any large quantities of technically sophisticated Hamas weapons, and would have destroyed these stashes before or during the first day of the attack. It is also improbable that Netanyahu would have risked an attack just on the eve of an election if Hamas possessed weapons capable of inflicting significant civilian casualties. A handful of Hamas projectiles did reach deeper inside Israel than previously, but these lacked explosives; an Israeli official derisively dismissed them as "pipes, basically."[7] If Israel ballyhooed Iron Dome, it was because its purported effectiveness was the only achievement to which Israel could point in the final reckoning.[8]

The last act of Pillar of Defense came when Israel hit up against a tactical dead end. On the one hand, it had struck all preplanned military targets but, on the other, it couldn't directly target the civilian population. Hamas had successfully adapted Hezbollah's strategy of continually firing its projectiles, the psychological upshot of which was that Israel couldn't declare its deterrence capacity had been restored, forcing on it a ground invasion to stop the projectile attacks. Israel could not, however, launch such an invasion without suffering heavy combatant losses, unless it blasted everyone and everything in and out of sight as it cleared a path into Gaza. But, because of the novel circumstances—the regional realignment after the Arab Spring, and Turkey under Erdoğan; the threat of a "mega-Goldstone," as an Israeli commentator put it;[9] the presence of a foreign press corps embedded not in the Israel Defense Forces but among the people of Gaza—Israel couldn't launch a murderous Cast Lead–style ground invasion. It was caught between the proverbial rock and a hard place. It couldn't subdue

Hamas without a ground invasion, but it couldn't launch a ground invasion without incurring either a domestically unacceptable price of combatant casualties or a diplomatically unacceptable price of global opprobrium and ostracism.

One can pinpoint the exact moment when Pillar of Defense collapsed. At a 19 November 2012 press conference, Hamas leader Khalid Mishal effectively told Netanyahu, *Go Ahead, Invade!* "If you wanted to launch it," he taunted, "you would have done it."[10] The Israeli prime minister panicked, his bluff had been called. What happened next was a repeat of the 2006 Israeli invasion of Lebanon. Unable to stop Hezbollah rocket attacks but dreading the prospect of a full-blown ground invasion that meant hand-to-hand combat with the Party of God, Israel had called in Secretary of State Condoleezza Rice to negotiate a cease-fire. This time, US Secretary of State Hillary Clinton was summoned by Netanyahu to bail Israel out. Not even the 21 November 2012 bus bombing in Tel Aviv—which, cease-fire or no cease-fire, would normally have elicited massive Israeli retaliation—shook the prime minister from his resolve to end Pillar of Defense immediately, before Hamas resumed its verbal digs.

The formal terms of the final agreement marked a stunning reversal for Israel. It called for a *mutual* cease-fire, not one, as Israel demanded, unilaterally imposed on Hamas. It also incorporated language implying that the siege of Gaza would be lifted. Notably, it did not include the precondition that Hamas must cease its importation or manufacture of weapons. The reason why is not hard to find. Under international law, peoples resisting foreign occupation are not debarred from using armed force.[11] Egypt, which brokered the cease-fire, was not about to barter away Hamas's legal right.[12] Israel undoubtedly anticipated that Washington would use its political leverage to extract better cease-fire terms from Cairo. But the Obama administration, hoping to bring the new Egypt under its wing, prioritized American interests and consequently was not willing to (assuming it could) lord it over Egypt on Israel's behalf.

If any doubt remained about who won and who lost in the new round, it was quickly dispelled. Israel launched Pillar of Defense to restore Gaza's fear of it. But after the cease-fire and its terms were announced, Palestinians flooded the streets of Gaza in a celebratory mood as if at a wedding party. In a CNN interview with

Christiane Amanpour, Hamas's Mishal cut the figure and exuded the confidence of a world leader. Meanwhile, at the Israeli press conference announcing the cease-fire, the ruling triumvirate—Netanyahu, Defense Minister Ehud Barak and Foreign Minister Avigdor Lieberman—resembled grade-schoolers called down to the Principal's Office, counting the seconds until the humiliation was over.

The cease-fire is likely to hold until and unless Israel can figure out how to militarily prevail in the new political environment. The days of Cast Lead are over, whereas a Pillar of Defense–type operation will not bear the fruits of victory. It is unlikely, however, that Israel will fulfill the terms of the final agreement to lift the siege of Gaza. During Israeli cabinet deliberations on whether or not to accept the cease-fire, Barak had already cynically dismissed the fine print, scoffing, "A day after the cease-fire, no one will remember what is written in that draft."[13]

Moreover, Egypt will probably not pressure the US to enforce the cease-fire terms on Israel. The respective interests of the new Egypt and Hamas mostly diverge, not converge. Egypt desperately needs American subventions and is currently negotiating a $5 billion loan from the International Monetary Fund, where Washington's vote is decisive. The popularity of President Mohammed Morsi's Muslim Brotherhood government will ultimately hinge on what it delivers to Egyptians, not Gazans. In the meantime, US political elites are lauding Morsi to high heaven, stroking his ego, and speculating on the "special relationship" he has cultivated with Obama. Those familiar with the psychological manipulations of Washington when it comes to Arab leaders—in particular, contemptibly mediocre ones, such as Anwar Sadat—will not be surprised by the current US romancing of Morsi. It is equally unlikely that Turkey will exert itself on Hamas's behalf. Right now, Ankara is smarting from Obama's rebuff of designating not itself but Cairo as prime interlocutor in brokering the cease-fire. (Turkey was apparently disqualified because it labeled Israel a "terrorist state" during the assault.[14]) Still, aspiring to be the US's preeminent regional partner, and calculating that the road to Washington passes through Tel Aviv, Turkey has resumed negotiations with Israel to break the diplomatic logjam after Israel's lethal assault on the *Mavi Marmara* in 2010.[15] On the other side, its recent operation has brought home to Israel that alienating both its historic allies in the region, Egypt and Turkey, is not prudent policy, so a face-saving reconciliation between Ankara and Tel Aviv (the Turkish government is formally demanding an apology, monetary compensation, and an end to the Gaza siege) is probably in the offing. The long and the short of it is that, even in the new era that has opened up, definite limits exist on how much regional support the Palestinians can realistically hope to garner.

Many Palestinians have inferred from the resounding defeat inflicted on Israel that only armed resistance can and will end the Israeli occupation. In fact, however, Hamas's armed resistance operated for the most part only at the level of perceptions—the projectiles heading towards Tel Aviv did unsettle the city's residents—while it is improbable that Palestinians can ever muster sufficient military might to compel an end to the occupation. But Gaza's steadfastness until the final hour of Operation Pillar of Defense did demonstrate the indomitable *will* of the people of Palestine. If this potential force can be harnessed in a campaign of mass civil resistance, and if the supporters of Palestinian rights worldwide do their

job of mobilizing public opinion and changing government policy, then Israel can be coerced into ending the
occupation, and with fewer Palestinian lives lost than in
armed resistance.

6/   ISRAEL HAS THE RIGHT TO DEFEND ITSELF (2014)

UNLIKE ISRAEL'S ATTACKS on Lebanon in 2006 (Second Lebanon War) and Gaza in 2008–9 (Operation Cast Lead), Operation Protective Edge, beginning 8 July 2014, was not preplanned long in advance.[1] It resulted from contingent factors, although many of its facets—Israeli provocations and annihilating force—conformed to a decades-old pattern. At the end of April 2014, the two leading Palestinian political factions, Hamas and Fatah, formed a "consensus government." Surprisingly, the US and European Union (EU) did not suspend engagement but, instead, adopted a wait-and-see approach, effectively legitimizing it. In part, they wanted to penalize Israel for aborting the "peace" initiative of US Secretary of State John Kerry. But Hamas had also made an unprecedented concession. It didn't oppose President Mahmoud Abbas when, speaking for the new government, he reiterated his support for the three negotiating preconditions set

forth by the US and EU: recognition of Israel, renuncia-
tion of violence, recognition of past agreements. Israeli
Prime Minister Benjamin Netanyahu erupted in a rage.[2]
He could no longer maintain the alibi that Abbas represented only some Palestinians, and that Hamas was a terrorist organization bent on Israel's destruction. His fury
was all the more unrestrained because the US and EU had
already ignored his dire prognostications by entering
into talks with Iran, which was supposedly threatening
Israel with a "second Holocaust."

In early June 2014, a gift dropped in Netanyahu's lap:
the abduction and killing by Palestinians of three Israeli
teenagers in the West Bank. It appears that Netanyahu
knew almost immediately that the teenagers had been
killed rather than abducted for purposes of a prisoner
exchange and that Hamas's leadership was not responsible.[3] But he decided to exploit the opportunity presented
by the abduction to destroy the Palestinian unity government. Feigning a rescue mission, Israel launched in
mid-June Operation Brother's Keeper in the West Bank,
killing at least five Palestinians, ransacking and demol-
ishing homes and businesses, and arresting some 700
Palestinians, mostly Hamas members, including many

who had been released in a 2011 prisoner exchange deal.[4] The rampage was transparently designed to evoke a violent response from Hamas so as to "prove" it was a terrorist organization, not to be trusted. Netanyahu then could, and in fact later did, scold the US, "never second-guess me again": *Didn't I tell you Hamas was a terrorist organization?*[5] Initially, Hamas resisted the Israeli provocations, although other Gaza factions did fire projectiles, but in the ensuing tit-for-tat, Hamas entered the fray and the violence spun out of control.[6]

Once hostilities broke out, Israel faced a dilemma familiar to it from the 2006 Lebanon war and Cast Lead. Short-range projectiles of the kind Hamas[7] possessed couldn't be disabled from the air; they had to be taken out at ground level. But a ground invasion would have cost Netanyahu either too much domestically, if many Israeli soldiers were killed fighting street-by-street with Hamas, or too much internationally, if Israeli soldiers immunized themselves from attack by laying waste Gaza's civilian infrastructure and killing many civilians as they advanced. Netanyahu consequently held back from launching a ground invasion, but then two more gifts dropped in his lap.

First, Tony Blair helped coordinate a cease-fire deal, formally presented by Egyptian strongman Abdel Fattah el-Sisi on 14 July, in which Hamas would agree to stop firing projectiles in exchange for an easing of the blockade when "the security situation stabilizes."[8] No such security caveat was stipulated in the two prior cease-fire agreements between Israel and Hamas in 2008 and 2012.[9] Inasmuch as Israel designates Hamas a terrorist organization, by definition the security situation in Gaza could stabilize only when Hamas was either defeated or disarmed itself, in the absence of which the illegal and inhuman siege would continue. It was surely known in advance that Hamas had to reject these cease-fire terms, which would then hand Israel a credible rationale for a brutal ground invasion. Second, the downing on 17 July of the Malaysian airliner over the Ukraine displaced Gaza as the headline news story. Here was an opportunity Netanyahu couldn't resist. After the 1989 Tiananmen Square massacre, which occurred during the first Palestinian uprising (intifada), Netanyahu reportedly declared that Israel had committed a blunder when it didn't expel "five, 50 or 500" Palestinian "inciters" from the occupied territories while media attention was riveted on China.[10] The downed airliner was Netanyahu's "Tiananmen moment." Realizing that he could inflict massive death and destruction, Netanyahu launched the ground invasion hours later, on the night of that very day.

Already before the ground invasion began, Israel had apparently exhausted its bank of military targets in Gaza and proceeded to outright terror bombing, which, as Israeli troops crossed the border, escalated into precision terror strikes on homes and businesses, schools and mosques, hospitals and ambulances, power stations and sewage plants, civilian shelters and fleeing citizens. Per usual, to justify the rising death toll, Israel accused Hamas of using civilians as "human shields"; per usual, reputable human rights organizations and journalists found no evidence to support Israel's allegation.[11] The obvious purpose of Israel's terror strikes was to subvert the will to resist of Gaza's civilian population, or turn it against Hamas either amid the fighting or after a cease-fire, when the dust had settled and Gazans took in the magnitude of the devastation. "I've never seen such massive destruction ever before," Peter Maurer, the president of the International Committee of the Red Cross, observed after touring the ravaged strip, while UN

Secretary-General Ban Ki-moon declared before the UN General Assembly, "The massive deaths and destruction in Gaza have shocked and shamed the world."[12]

Operation Protective Edge did not turn out quite as Netanyahu anticipated. In some respects it fared better, but in other respects worse. He did get *carte blanche* from the White House to pulverize Gaza. It was manifest from early on that Israel was targeting or firing indiscriminately at civilians and civilian infrastructure.[13] Even Human Rights Watch (HRW), which routinely provides legal cover for Israel,[14] had to concede that Israel was probably committing war crimes.[15] But, despite some behind-the-scenes tensions,[16] Washington did not publicly exert pressure on Israel to desist; on the contrary, each day President Obama or his spokespersons, intoning Israel's "right to self-defense" and refusing to condemn Israeli atrocities, gave Netanyahu the green light to continue.[17] It ought never to be forgotten that Obama was the enabler-in-chief of Israel's latest massacre. It might be asked, *Why did the*

Obama administration back Israel's assault if it supported negotiations with the unity government? The answer is, once Hamas projectiles started flying over Israel, and Israel's domestic lobby lined up wall-to-wall Congressional support,[18] it would have taken spine for Obama to defy it, which he lacks. Still, did he really have to reaffirm Israel's "right to defend itself" day in and day out, even as human rights organizations documented Israeli war crimes?

Meanwhile, in recent years the balance of forces elsewhere has dramatically shifted in Israel's favor. Netanyahu benefited hugely from this political realignment during Protective Edge. Regional powers, such as Egypt and Saudi Arabia, openly longed for Hamas's removal from power.[19] The Arab League—in its sole meeting on Gaza—even supported the cynical Egyptian cease-fire ultimatum.[20] Only Iran, Turkey, and Qatar among Middle Eastern powers opposed the Israeli attack. A critical factor limiting the damage Israel wreaked during Operation Pillar of Defense (2012) was the strong backing Egypt and Turkey lent Hamas.[21] But after the July 2013 coup Egypt became Hamas's sworn nemesis, while Turkey was preoccupied with other regional developments, notably in Syria.

Convulsed by its own internal conflicts and humanitarian crises, the so-called street across large swaths of the Arab world fell mute during the Israeli assault. As a result, corrupt Arab dictators and their Washington backer paid no price for egging on Israel. The EU also gave Israel a free pass because it dreaded "militant Islam," now spreading like wildfire under the ISIS banner, to which Hamas was, rightly or wrongly (in this writer's opinion, wrongly), assimilated. The only notable exceptions outside the Middle East were Latin American states (Argentina, Bolivia, Brazil, El Salvador, Chile, Peru, Uruguay, Venezuela), which, in a rare display of selfless solidarity with beleaguered Gaza, registered diplomatically their disgust at Israeli actions.[22] Still, amidst the slaughter, Gaza basically stood alone and abandoned.

A less welcome surprise for Israel was the sophisticated, ramified network of tunnels that Hamas had dug inside Gaza. Adopting and adapting Hezbollah's strategy during the 2006 Lebanon war, the Palestinian resistance used projectiles to lure Israel into a ground invasion, and then emerged from tunnels, which withstood Israeli aerial bombing and artillery shells, to inflict an unprecedented number of combatant casualties.[23]

Only ten Israeli soldiers were killed in Cast Lead, four by friendly fire; many Israeli soldiers testified not having even seen a Hamas fighter.[24] This time around, however, at least 66 Israeli soldiers were killed. Because of so many combatant deaths, advancing Israeli troops marked time, never penetrating more than 2–3 kilometers beyond the border.[25] Israel abruptly recalibrated its mission from destroying Hamas "rockets" to destroying Hamas "terror tunnels" exiting on its side of the border. But, of the 32 tunnels Israel allegedly discovered and detonated, only 12 passed under the border,[26] while Israel could easily have sealed them from its side, just as Egypt after the July coup sealed some one thousand tunnels passing from Gaza into the Sinai. Israel's actual goal was to destroy the tunnels *inside* Gaza so that, when it next had to "mow the grass," Hamas fighters wouldn't again be able to inflict heavy combatant casualties. By proclaiming a "right" to destroy the tunnel system, Israel was effectively saying that Palestinians had no right to defend themselves against Israel's periodic massacres. Even if Netanyahu did seek to destroy tunnels used by Hamas infiltrators, it's hard to figure out why this would be legitimate. Do the laws of war prescribe that planes, artillery shells, and tanks get to breach Gaza's border at Israel's will and whim, but Palestinian tunnels must not violate Israel's sacred space?

Israel not only misrepresented the nature of the threat posed by Hamas's "terror tunnels." It also misrepresented the threat posed by Hamas's "rockets." Although Hamas allegedly fired some 3,900 rockets at Israel, they caused only seven civilian casualties and $15 million in property damage.[27] The vast discrepancy between the scale of the attack and its material consequences is supposedly reconciled by the miracle of the Iron Dome antimissile defense system. This explanation, however, is not plausible. Israel suffered only three civilian casualties and (in an odd coincidence) $15 million in property damage during Cast Lead—that is, before Iron Dome came along.[28] It might still be argued, in support of Iron Dome's efficacy, that Hamas fired far fewer "rockets" (925) during Cast Lead. But Israel's early warning sirens and shelters have been markedly improved since Cast Lead; if Hamas fired more rockets this time around and Israel suffered roughly the same losses as in 2008–9, that just as well might be chalked up to the overhaul of its civil defense system.

The bigger point, however, is this: For many years before Cast Lead, the blockade of Gaza was sufficiently porous for relatively sophisticated rockets to be smuggled in from Hamas's benefactor in Iran. But just before and then after Cast Lead, the blockade of Gaza was gradually tightened. The tunnel system with Egypt somewhat compensated, and weapons no doubt still made their way in. However, (1) Hamas's stash of rockets was depleted in 2012 during Operation Pillar of Defense, (2) Iran downgraded relations with Hamas in 2013 after it realigned against Syrian strongman (and Iranian ally) Bashar al-Assad, and (3) after the military coup in Egypt, the new regime sealed nearly all the tunnels between Gaza and Egypt. In broad strokes, then, and allowing for the occasional exception, the picture prior to Protective Edge was this: Hamas had no rockets in its armory, no allies from whom to acquire them, no way to smuggle them in, and no wherewithal to manufacture them. The notion that Hamas fired thousands of rockets at Israel (and had thousands more still hidden away), while it was the miracle of Iron Dome that spared Israel from devastation, is almost certainly a fiction. Dismissing Israel's Iron Dome hoopla, MIT missile defense expert Theodore

Postol estimated that fewer than ten percent of Iron Dome's intercepts were successful, and he ascribed the fewness of Israeli civilian casualties to its sophisticated civil defense system and the smallness of the warheads on Hamas "rockets" (10- to 20-pound range).[29] But this hypothesis would not yet account for the minimal infrastructural damage Israel witnessed: if Iron Dome did not disable 3,500 (of the 3,900) incoming Hamas rockets, wouldn't total property damage from even small warheads exceed $15 million? The only plausible explanation is that Hamas "rockets" consisted overwhelmingly of enhanced fireworks.

Initially, Israel grossly inflated the threat posed by Hamas's projectiles to justify its campaign of terror bombing. However, its pretext backfired when the projectiles kept coming and, among other things, Israel's tourism industry took a big hit.[30] When a Hamas projectile landed in the vicinity of Ben-Gurion Airport, prompting international airlines to suspend flights to Israel, former New York City mayor Michael Bloomberg obligingly flew over in order to reassure prospective travelers.[31] But if all was well in Israel because of Iron Dome, then why was Israel pulverizing Gaza? Not missing a beat, Israel conjured a new rationale, quickly aped by credulous and apologetic journalists: Hamas's "terror tunnels," which "exist solely to annihilate our civilians and to kill our children" (Netanyahu). But this pretext also backfired when Israeli evacuees recoiled at the prospect of returning to their border communities. So, some Israelis eventually conceded that the targets of Hamas fighters infiltrating via tunnels were Israeli soldiers, not civilians.[32] Spewing forth one lie after another, Israel kept catching itself in the tangled web of its deceits. The miracle of Iron Dome also provided Israelis with psychological solace. Israel first boasted of its success after Pillar of Defense when Gazans flooded the streets celebrating victory against the invading army. Israel's purported technical ingenuity served to compensate, then and now, for its failure to inflict a decisive military defeat on Hamas. Israel's flourishing arms trade also stood to reap rich dividends from Iron Dome's bogus advertising.

Israel's targeting of UN schools, which HRW later found to be "war crimes," killed scores of Gazans seeking refuge and eventually evoked international outrage.[33] Even normally comatose US puppet Ban Ki-moon finally denounced one of these atrocities as a "moral outrage and criminal act."[34] Totally isolated on the world stage, the Obama administration itself joined in the chorus of condemnation. Notwithstanding Obama's abrupt reversal, Israel's Congressional cheerleaders went mute: defending Israel internationally had become too heavy a burden to bear, as it undermined the US "national interest." Immediately after Washington declared on 3 August that it was "appalled" by Israel's "disgraceful" shelling of a UN school sheltering civilians,[35] Netanyahu announced that Israeli troops were withdrawing. But another factor also came into play. Israel could only proceed with the ground invasion if it ventured into Gaza's built-up areas. To avoid street-by-street fighting and concomitant combatant casualties, Israel would have to blast everything in sight, causing many thousands of civilian deaths, which international public opinion would not abide, and, even then, Israel would still suffer heavy combatant losses as Hamas fighters popped out of the tunnels.[36] To cover up for its failure to destroy Hamas's catacombs, Israel proclaimed that it had destroyed nearly all of Hamas's "known" tunnels.[37]

Across the official political spectrum, a broad consensus crystallized on two points: Israel had the right to defend itself and Hamas had to be disarmed. For argument's sake, let's set aside the curiosity that Israel was said to be defending itself although it initiated the armed hostilities, while Hamas was called upon to disarm although it was acting in self-defense. Instead, let's juxtapose these consensus beliefs with the relevant norms of international law.

International law prohibits an occupying power from using force to suppress a struggle for self-determination, whereas it does *not* prohibit a people struggling for self-determination from using force.[38] The International Court of Justice (ICJ) stated in a 2004 advisory opinion that the Palestinian people's "rights include the right to self-determination," and that "Israel is bound to comply with its obligation to respect the right of the Palestinian people to self-determination."[39] Israel consequently has no legal mandate to use force to suppress the Palestinian self-determination struggle. Israel also cannot contend that, because this self-determination struggle unfolds within the framework of an occupation, it has the legal right, as the occupying power, to enforce the occupation so long as it endures.[40] In 1971, the ICJ ruled that South Africa's occupation of Namibia had become illegal because it refused to carry out good-faith negotiations to end the occupation. It is beyond dispute that Israel has failed to carry out good-faith negotiations to end the occupation of Palestinian territory. On the Namibia precedent, the Israeli occupation is also illegal.[41] The only "right" Israel can claim is—in the words of the US at the time of the Namibia debate—"to withdraw its administration . . . immediately and thus put an end to its occupation."

Although claiming for itself the right of self-defense against Hamas projectiles, in fact Israel is claiming the right to maintain the occupation. If Israel ceased using force to suppress the Palestinian struggle for self-determination, the occupation would end, and the projectile attacks would cease. (If they didn't stop, the legal situation would, of course, be different.) Put otherwise, if it ended the occupation, Israel wouldn't need to use force. The refrain that Israel has the right to self-defense is a red herring. The real question is, *Does Israel have the right to use force to maintain an illegal occupation?* The answer is no.

It might be said that, even if Israel cannot use force to suppress the Palestinian struggle for self-determination, Hamas's use of indiscriminate projectiles and its targeting of Israeli civilians still amount to war crimes. But it is not altogether clear what constitutes an indiscriminate weapon. The apparent standard is a relative one set by cutting-edge technology: If an existing weapon has a high probability of hitting its target, then any weapons with a significantly lower probability are classified as indiscriminate. But, by this standard, only rich countries, or countries rich enough to purchase high-tech weapons, have a right to defend themselves against high-tech aerial assaults. It is a peculiar law that would negate the raison d'être of law: the substitution of might by right.

It is often alleged that, even if its civilians are being relentlessly targeted, a people does not have a legal right to carry out "belligerent reprisals"—that is, to deliberately target the civilians of the opposing state until it desists. "Regardless of who started this latest round, attacks targeting civilians violate basic humanitarian norms," HRW asserted right after armed hostilities broke out. "All attacks, including reprisal attacks, that target or indiscriminately harm civilians are prohibited under the laws of war, period."[42] Not so. International law does not—at any rate, not yet—prohibit belligerent reprisals.[43] The US and Britain, among others, have staunchly defended the right of a state to use even *nuclear* weapons by way of belligerent reprisals.[44] By this standard, the people of Gaza surely have the right to use makeshift projectiles to end an illegal, merciless seven-year-long Israeli blockade or to end Israel's criminal bombardment. Indeed, in its landmark 1996 advisory opinion on the legality of nuclear weapons, the ICJ ruled that international law is not settled on the right of a state to use nuclear weapons when its "survival" is at stake. But, if a state might have the right to use nuclear weapons when its survival is at stake, then surely a *people* struggling for self-determination has the right to use makeshift projectiles when its survival is at stake.

One might legitimately question the political prudence of Hamas's strategy. But the law is not unambiguously against it, while the scales of morality weigh in its favor. Israel has imposed a brutal blockade on Gaza. Fully 95 percent of the water in Gaza is unfit for human consumption. By all accounts, the Palestinian people stood behind those engaging in belligerent reprisals against

Israel. In the Gaza Strip, they preferred to die resisting rather than continue living under an inhuman blockade.[45] Their resistance is mostly notional, as the makeshift projectiles caused little damage. So, the ultimate question is, *Do Palestinians have the right to symbolically resist slow death punctuated by periodic massacres, or is it incumbent upon them to lie down and die?*

CONCLUSION (2014)

OPERATION PROTECTIVE EDGE DRAGGED ON three more weeks after Prime Minister Benjamin Netanyahu announced the end of the ground offensive. He still harbored hopes of inflicting a decisive defeat on Hamas by attrition through massive aerial bombardments, massive civilian casualties, and the assassination of senior Hamas military leaders. Because Western media attention, after the beheading of an American journalist, shifted to ISIS, and the Gaza massacre entered the ho-hum, more-of-the-same phase of the news cycle, Israel was able to resume the precision terror strikes with unprecedented abandon, flattening high-rise apartment buildings, as if playing a video game and with barely a pretense that they constituted legitimate military objectives.[1] But the Hamas projectiles and mortar shells kept coming, causing Israeli civilian casualties to mount. On 26 August 2014, a cease-fire went into effect.

By massacre's end, Israel had killed 2,200 Palestinians, of whom 70–75 percent were civilians. Among the dead were 500 Palestinian children. In addition, 11,000 Palestinians suffered injuries (including 3,300 children, of whom 1,000 will be permanently disabled); 11,000 homes, 360 factories and workshops, 160 mosques, 100 schools, and 10 hospitals were either destroyed or severely damaged; 100,000 Palestinians were left homeless.[2] Israel suffered at least 66 combatant and five civilian casualties (a foreign guest worker was also killed). Among the dead was one Israeli child. In addition, 120 Israelis suffered injuries (one person was seriously wounded).

The essential terms of the cease-fire required Israel (and Egypt) to ease the blockade of Gaza. The Palestinian Authority (PA), headed by President Mahmoud Abbas, would administer the border crossings, coordinate the international reconstruction effort, and was expected to prevent weapons from entering Gaza. Other points of contention (e.g., release of Palestinian prisoners, construction of an airport and seaport in Gaza) were deferred to future negotiations.[3]

At a news conference after the cease-fire had been reached, Netanyahu boasted of Israel's "great military and political achievement."[4] In fact, Israel did not achieve any of its avowed aims. Initially, Netanyahu's goal was to fracture the Palestinian unity government by once more demonizing Hamas as a terrorist organization. But the unity government held together, although Abbas no doubt secretly longed for Israel to deliver Hamas a death blow. If Israel hoped to prove that Hamas was a terrorist organization, it ended up convincing many more people that Israel was a terrorist state. If Israel hoped to convince the US and EU not to negotiate with a unity government that included Hamas, it ended up itself negotiating with the unity government and indirectly even with Hamas. "Effectively," an influential Israeli columnist observed, "Israel has recognized Hamas."[5] Once hostilities escalated, Netanyahu's avowed goal was to destroy Hamas's "rockets" and "terror tunnels." But Israel was unable to fully realize either of these objectives: Hamas kept firing rockets and mortar shells (killing two Israelis in the last hour before the cease-fire), while an unknown number of tunnels remained intact. Israel's broader, tacit goal of inflicting a comprehensive military and political defeat on Hamas also went unfulfilled. Although Israel made any concessions conditional on Hamas's disarmament, the cease-fire agreement did not require the Islamic resistance to lay down its weapons, and only a vague promise was extracted from the PA to stem the flow of arms into Gaza. The cease-fire's terms "didn't include any statement, not even a hint, regarding Israel's security demands," an Israeli diplomatic correspondent groused. "There was nothing about the demilitarization of the strip, the rearming or the issue of the tunnels."[6] Despite being the regional superpower, Israel "failed to impose its will on an isolated enemy operating in a besieged territory without advanced weaponry."[7] Such an inglorious outcome could not but undermine Israel's sacred "deterrence capacity"—i.e., its ability to terrify potential regional rivals into submission. Ironically, the chief beneficiary of this latest Gaza massacre was Lebanon. After its military fiasco, Israel will think twice before attacking Hezbollah, which possesses a formidable arsenal of real, sophisticated rockets,[8] reducing Iron Dome's potential efficacy quotient from ten percent to near zero, and a tunnel network dug deep inside mountains. In a replay of the aftermath of Operation Pillar of Defense, Israel's Prime Minister, Defense Minister, and Chief of Staff cut sorry figures at the news conference proclaiming Israel's

"victory" in Protective Edge.[9] Netanyahu's one unqual-
ified achievement was to satiate the bloodlust of Israeli
society that he himself whipped up. Rubbing their hands
in undisguised glee, many Israelis relished the prospect
of Gazans confronting, once the soot had settled, the
massive death and destruction Israel had visited on them.

Hamas also claimed victory.[10] Once hostilities broke
out, its primary goal was to end the blockade of Gaza.
Whereas the original Egyptian cease-fire proposal
stipulated that the siege would be lifted only after "the
security situation stabilizes" in Gaza, the final cease-fire
agreement omitted this condition. However, it called
only for the blockade to be eased (not lifted) and did not
include an external enforcement mechanism. In effect,
it reinstated the cease-fire terms that ended Operation
Pillar of Defense (2012), which Israel had then proceeded
to ignore. Hamas apparently settled for less because of
Israel's relentless devastation. "Our demands were just,"
Hamas leader Khalid Mishal told a news conference, "but
in the end we had the Palestinian demands on the one
hand and the pain of Gaza's civilian population on the
other."[11] "We agreed to the cease-fire," Mishal continued,
"in the knowledge that the siege will be lifted," but, based

on Israel's past performance, this seems wishful thinking unless Hamas disarms or is unable to rearm.[12] If Gazans flocked into the streets to celebrate after the cease-fire was declared, it was to proclaim, firstly to themselves and then to the world, that, however enormous the toll, however great the sacrifice, the people of Palestine still live. *We were, we are, we will be!*

As hostilities wound down, Netanyahu gestured to the possibility of a final agreement with Palestinians. He spoke of a "new diplomatic horizon" and beckoned Abbas to join him.[13] If he meant accepting US Secretary of State John Kerry's recent initiative, the PA would jump at such a prospect, and indeed is being groomed for it. It has been delegated the dual task of preventing Hamas from rearming, in order to clear away any political obstacle to a deal, and supervising international reconstruction of Gaza, in order to enhance its financial authority—i.e., capacity to dole out bribes—among Gazans. The US and EU would surely also leap at an end to the conflict. But the odds are against such a deal materializing. The maximum that could come of this process would be Kerry's parameters, which amount to a thinly disguised Palestinian surrender.[14] Still, in Israel's current vengeful mood, licking its wounds from the military debacle, even if he so desired (which is doubtful), Netanyahu couldn't sell anything short of total Israeli victory/abject Palestinian defeat to the Israeli public and, in particular, his political base. On the other side, Abbas will not be able to disarm Hamas if only because corrupt PA-Egyptian security forces stationed at the Rafah border crossing can be paid off to turn a blind eye as arms trickle in. Nor will he be able to impose a Palestinian surrender after the resurgence of Hamas's popularity.[15] Meanwhile, the US is preoccupied elsewhere in the region, Obama's term of office is coming to an end, and, after having had his fingers burnt so many times by Netanyahu, he probably won't risk any more political capital unless Israel sends an unambiguous and unequivocal signal—which it won't—that it's ready to settle.[16] The bottom line is, Palestinians cannot even hope for an unjust deal, let alone a just deal, through diplomacy.

Judicial recourse also doesn't hold much promise. The UN Human Rights Council appointed a fact-finding mission "to investigate purported violations of international humanitarian and human rights law ... since the conflict began on 13 June."[17] The head of the mission,

William Schabas, although a consistent critic of Israeli violations of international law, is privately reputed to be a vainglorious personality accommodating to power, much like his predecessor Richard Goldstone (Schabas is part Jewish). It doesn't bode well in the face of an inevitable US-Israeli juggernaut opposing the mission; Israel has already launched a preemptive campaign to delegitimize Schabas.[18] The PA (alongside members of the Arab League) helped kill the Goldstone Report in the Human Rights Council[19] and, if called upon, it will almost certainly do so again. The PA is additionally being pressured by its own public, as well as human rights organizations and prominent legal scholars, to seek legal redress at the International Criminal Court (ICC). Even if, despite US-EU opposition,[20] the PA does manage to access the Rome Statute of the ICC,[21] the possibility remains remote that Israel's leaders will ever be indicted for war crimes. The tacit axiom of the ICC is that only nonwhites commit heinous acts warranting prosecution; to date, it has only indicted Africans. The ICC mindset can be gleaned from comments of its former chief prosecutor. On a recent visit to Israel, Luis Moreno-Ocampo heaped praise on Israel's legal system, its respect for the "rule of law," and its "great lawyers."[22] Indeed, who dares cast doubt on a judicial system that legalized torture and hostage taking?[23] Meanwhile, the PA, in thrall to Washington, will not venture beyond using the prospect of an ICC indictment to extract political concessions from Israel,[24] and Hamas, although officially supporting ICC intervention, no doubt fears its own vulnerability in this venue. In short, judging by the fate of the Goldstone Report and Turkey's attempt to hold Israel accountable after the *Mavi Marmara* massacre, as well as by the built-in biases of the ICC, the legal route is almost certainly a cul-de-sac.

If diplomacy and judicial redress won't go anywhere, then the only option left is popular resistance. But what *kind* of popular resistance? The question is not whether Palestinians have the right to use armed force to end the occupation. Of course, they do. Rather, the point at issue is a practical one: *Which tactics and strategy are most likely to yield political gains?* However heroic the resistance of the people of Gaza, however inspiring their indomitable will, the fact remains that, after going three bloody rounds with Israel in the past five years, after suffering death and destruction on a heartrending scale, armed resistance has yet to produce substantive improvements in people's daily lives.

What if the quantum of time, energy, creativity and ingenuity channeled into building the tunnels (a wondrous feat of civil engineering) were instead invested in Gaza's most precious resource: *the people*? What if they organized a mass nonviolent demonstration demanding an end to the blockade of Gaza? What if 1.8 million Gazans marched on the Israeli border crossings under the banner, STOP STRANGLING US! END THE ILLEGAL BLOCKADE OF GAZA! What if Gaza's one million children stood at the head of the march? Yes, *children*. Wasn't it the "children's miracle" in Selma, Alabama, during the Civil Rights Movement that broke the back of segregation, when Black children, positioned in the front lines, fended off police attack dogs and high-velocity fire hoses?[25] What if Palestinians found the inner wherewithal to stay nonviolent even as Israel fired murderously on the crowd? What if the vast reservoir of Palestine's international supporters simultaneously converged, in the *hundreds of thousands*, on UN headquarters in New York and Geneva, enveloping and blockading the buildings?

Wouldn't Ban Ki-moon (or whatever US minion happens to be holding office) be forced to denounce the Israeli bloodbath, just as he did on 3 August when Israel destroyed the UN shelter filled with children? Wouldn't Washington, isolated on the world stage, then be forced to denounce Israeli atrocities, just as it did on 3 August? Wouldn't Israel then be politically cornered, just as Netanyahu was on 3 August when he suspended the ground invasion? Long before Israel killed 2,200 Palestinians, 500 of them children, it's quite possible, judging by the sequence of events on 3 August, that mass nonviolent resistance can end the blockade if, in one last exertion of will, Palestinians find the strength to sacrifice, and the rest of us flood the streets surrounding the UN, ready to risk arrest and injury.

The best that can be said for armed resistance is that it has been tried many times to break the siege but failed. The worst that can be said for mass nonviolent resistance is that it hasn't yet been tried. Shouldn't it at least be given a chance?

CHRONOLOGY

1956   Outbreak of armed hostilities between Israel and Egypt

1967   Outbreak of armed hostilities between Israel and neighboring Arab states; Israel occupies West Bank, Gaza Strip, Sinai, Golan Heights

1982   Outbreak of armed hostilities between Israel and Lebanon; Israel occupies south Lebanon

1987   Outbreak of first intifada in the occupied Palestinian territories

1993   Israel, Palestinians sign Oslo Accord

2000   Israeli occupation forces evicted from south Lebanon

2000   Outbreak of second intifada in the occupied Palestinian territories

2005   Israel withdraws troops, settlers from inside Gaza

2006   Outbreak of armed hostilities between Israel and Lebanon

2006   Hamas wins Palestinian elections

2007   Hamas takes control of Gaza after preempting coup attempt

RECENT KEY EVENTS

June 2008	Israel, Hamas agree to Egyptian-brokered cease-fire
November 2008	Israel breaks cease-fire
December 2008	Israel launches Operation Cast Lead
January 2009	Mutual unilateral cease-fire
November 2012	Israel launches Operation Pillar of Defense
November 2012	Egyptian-brokered cease-fire
July 2014	Israel launches Operation Protective Edge
August 2014	Egyptian-brokered cease-fire

NOTES

1/ PEACE OFFENSIVE

1. Amira Hass, *Drinking the Sea at Gaza: Days and nights in a land under siege* (New York: 1996), p. 9.

2. Sara Roy, *Failing Peace: Gaza and the Palestinian-Israeli conflict* (London: 2007), pp. 327–28. See also Galia Golan, *Israel and Palestine: Peace plans from Oslo to disengagement* (Princeton: 2007), p. 119.

3. Human Rights Watch, "'Disengagement' Will Not End Gaza Occupation" (29 October 2004). HRW's *World Report 2006* reiterated this position:

    In August and September 2005, Israel unilaterally withdrew approximately eight thousand settlers, along with military personnel and installations, from the Gaza Strip and four small settlements in the northern West Bank near Jenin. While Israel has since declared the Gaza Strip a "foreign territory" and the crossings between Gaza and Israel "international borders," under international humanitarian law (IHL), Gaza remains occupied, and Israel retains its responsibilities for the welfare of Gaza residents. Israel maintains effective control over Gaza by regulating movement in and out of the Strip as well as the airspace, sea space, public utilities and population registry. In addition, Israel declared the right to re-enter Gaza militarily at any time in its "Disengagement

Plan." Since the withdrawal, Israel has carried out aerial bombardments, including targeted killings, and has fired artillery into the northeastern corner of Gaza.

For a detailed legal analysis, see Gisha (Legal Center for Freedom of Movement), *Disengaged Occupiers: The legal status of Gaza* (Tel Aviv: January 2007). The UN Human Rights Council Mission chaired by Richard Goldstone affirmed that Israel "exercised effective control over the Gaza Strip" and that "the circumstances of this control establish that the Gaza Strip remains occupied by Israel" (*Report of the United Nations Fact-Finding Mission on the Gaza Conflict* (25 September 2009) (hereafter: Goldstone Report), paras. 187, 276–79).

4. Yoram Dinstein, *The International Law of Belligerent Occupation* (Cambridge: 2009), p. 277.

5. "One of the most important 'achievements,'" of the Oslo Accord for Israel, and "of which Rabin was proud," was "the exclusion of specific language freezing settlement construction in the period of the interim arrangement" (Yossi Beilin, *The Path to Geneva: The quest for a permanent agreement, 1996–2004* (New York: 2004), p. 278). On the issue of settlements, see also B'Tselem (Israeli Information Center for Human Rights in the Occupied Territories), *Land Grab: Israel's settlement policy in the West Bank* (Jerusalem: May 2002). For the Oslo years generally, see Norman G. Finkelstein, *Knowing Too Much: Why the American Jewish romance with Israel is coming to an end* (New York: 2012), Chapters 5 and 9.

6. Jimmy Carter, *Palestine Peace Not Apartheid* (New York: 2006), pp. 159–60.

7. David Rose, "The Gaza Bombshell," *Vanity Fair* (April 2008); Paul McGeough, *Kill Khalid: The failed Mossad assassination of Khalid Mishal and the rise of Hamas* (New York: 2009),

pp. 349–82. See also International Institute for Strategic Studies, "Hamas Coup in Gaza" (June 2007).

8. Norman G. Finkelstein, *"This Time We Went Too Far": Truth and consequences of the Gaza invasion,* revised and expanded paperback edition (New York: 2011), pp. 16–17.

9. "Cast Lead" refers to a line in a Hanukkah song.

10. For background and analysis, see Mouin Rabbani, "Birth Pangs of a New Palestine," *Middle East Report Online* (7 January 2009; http://tinyurl.com/a2bu6l).

11. International Crisis Group, *Gaza's Unfinished Business* (April 2009), p. 21; see ibid., pp. 27–28, for the post-invasion cease-fire terms.

12. *Report of the Independent Fact-Finding Committee on Gaza: No safe place.* Presented to the League of Arab States (30 April 2009), para. 411(3). The Committee was chaired by eminent South African legal scholar John Dugard.

13. Amnesty International, *Operation "Cast Lead": 22 Days of death and destruction* (London: July 2009), p. 7; for details, see ibid., pp. 11ff. See also Goldstone Report, paras. 459, 653–703.

14. Amnesty International, *Operation "Cast Lead,"* pp. 1, 24; for details, see ibid., esp. pp. 24–27. See also Goldstone Report, paras. 704–885.

15. Human Rights Watch, *White Flag Deaths: Killings of Palestinian civilians during Operation Cast Lead* (New York: August 2009), pp. 2, 4, 10–15.

16. The State of Israel, *The Operation in Gaza, 27 December 2008–18 January 2009: Factual and legal aspects* (July 2009), para. 213; Asa Kasher, "A Moral Evaluation of the Gaza War," *Jerusalem Post* (7 February 2010).

17. Anshel Pfeffer, "Israel Claims Success in the PR War," *Jewish Chronicle* (31 December 2008); Hirsh Goodman, "Analysis: The

effective public diplomacy ended with Operation Cast Lead," *Jerusalem Post* (5 February 2009).

18. Anthony H. Cordesman, *The "Gaza War": A strategic analysis* (Washington, DC: 2 February 2009; "Final Review Draft"), pp. 31–32, 68. For an extensive critique of this publication, see Finkelstein, *"This Time,"* Chapter 3.

19. Bradley Burston, "Why Does the World Media Love to Hate Israel?," *Haaretz* (23 March 2009); Shlomo Avineri, "What Was the Computer Thinking?," *Haaretz* (18 March 2009). Heeding such counsel, Israel in its official brief avoided mentioning Cast Lead apart from a parenthetical reference to "the 'Gaza Operation,' also known as 'Operation Cast Lead'" (*Operation in Gaza*, para. 16).

20. Gideon Levy, "The Time of the Righteous," *Haaretz* (9 January 2009).

21. Ethan Bronner, "Israel Reminds Foes That It Has Teeth," *New York Times* (29 December 2008).

22. Benny Morris, "Why Israel Feels Threatened," *New York Times* (30 December 2008).

23. Benny Morris, *Righteous Victims: A history of the Zionist-Arab conflict, 1881–2001* (New York: 2001), p. 686.

24. Norman G. Finkelstein, *Knowing Too Much*, Chapter 7 (Johnson at p. 172).

25. "Memorandum for the Record" (1 June 1967), *Foreign Relations of the United States, 1964–1968,* vol. 19, *Arab-Israeli Crisis and War, 1967* (Washington, DC: 2004).

26. See Finkelstein, *Knowing Too Much*, Chapter 7 (esp. pp. 166–67).

27. Tom Segev, *1967: Israel, the war, and the year that transformed the Middle East* (New York: 2007), p. 293, my emphasis.

28. Zeev Maoz, *Defending the Holy Land: A critical analysis of Israel's security and foreign policy* (Ann Arbor: 2006), p. 89.

29. Matthew Kalman, "Israel Set War Plan More Than a Year Ago," *San Francisco Chronicle* (21 July 2006).

30. The Reut Institute, *Building a Political Firewall against Israel's Delegitimization* (Tel Aviv: March 2010), para. 35.

31. Yaron London, "The Dahiya Strategy" (6 October 2008; http://tinyurl.com/c7tdjv). Gabriel Siboni, "Disproportionate Force: Israel's concept of response in light of the Second Lebanon War," *Institute for National Security Studies* (INSS) (2 October 2008). Giora Eiland, "The Third Lebanon War: Target Lebanon," *Strategic Assessment* (November 2008). Amos Harel, "Analysis: IDF plans to use disproportionate force in next war," *Haaretz* (5 October 2007). Joseph Nasr, "Israel Warns Hezbollah War Would Invite Destruction," *Reuters* (2 October 2008).

32. London, "Dahiya Strategy." Attila Somfalvi, "Sheetrit: We should level Gaza neighborhoods" (2 October 2008; http://tinyurl.com/c264xn).

33. "Israeli General Says Hamas Must Not Be the Only Target in Gaza," IDF Radio, Tel Aviv, in Hebrew 0600 gmt (26 December 2008), BBC Monitoring Middle East; Tova Dadon, "Deputy Chief of Staff: Worst still ahead," *ynetnews.com* (29 December 2008; http://tinyurl.com/crwdbw); "B'Tselem to Attorney General Mazuz: Concern over Israel targeting civilian objects in the Gaza Strip" (31 December 2008; http://tinyurl.com/8gxwox); Goldstone Report, para. 1204. For more on the Dahiya strategy and the quote from Channel 10 News, see Public Committee Against Torture in Israel (PCATI), *No Second Thoughts: The changes in the Israeli Defense Forces' combat doctrine in light of "Operation Cast Lead"* (Jerusalem: November 2009), pp. 20–28.

34. Seumas Milne, "Israel's Onslaught on Gaza is a Crime That Cannot Succeed," *Guardian* (30 December 2008); Shay Fogelman, "Shock and Awe," *Haaretz* (31 December 2010).

35. Amnesty International, *Operation "Cast Lead,"* p. 47.

36. Reuven Pedatzur, "The Mistakes of Cast Lead," *Haaretz* (8 January 2009).

37. Morris, "Why Israel Feels Threatened"; Matt M. Matthews, "The Israeli Defense Forces Response to the 2006 War with Hezbollah," *Military Review* (July–August 2009), p. 45.

38. B. Michael, "Déjà Vu in Gaza," *ynetnews.com* (29 December 2008; http://tinyurl.com/d2r2v4).

39. Al Mezan Center for Human Rights, *Bearing the Brunt Again: Child rights violations during Operation Cast Lead* (September 2009), p. 28; Human Rights Watch, *Precisely Wrong: Gaza civilians killed by Israeli drone-launched missiles* (30 June 2009), pp. 14–17. HRW found that "no Palestinian fighters were active on the street or in the immediate area just prior to or at the time of the attack" on the college students.

40. International Crisis Group, *Ending the War in Gaza* (5 January 2009), p. 18.

41. Amos Harel and Avi Issacharoff, "Israel and Hamas Are Both Paying a Steep Price in Gaza," *Haaretz* (10 January 2009); Ari Shavit, "Analysis: Israel's victories in Gaza make up for its failures in Lebanon," *Haaretz* (12 January 2009); Guy Bechor, "A Dangerous Victory," *ynetnews.com* (12 January 2009; http://tinyurl.com/c7gn7e). Looking back a year later, Harel recalled that the Gaza invasion "was considered to be an effective remedy to the failures of the 2006 Second Lebanon War" (Amos Harel, "Israel Stuck in the Mud on Internal Gaza Probe," *Haaretz* (30 January 2010)). For a critique of Shavit's comments during the 2008–9 invasion (and his 2014 bestselling book), see Norman G. Finkelstein, *Old Wine, Broken Bottle: Ari Shavit's Promised Land* (New York: 2014), Chapter 4.

42. Thomas L. Friedman, "Israel's Goals in Gaza?," *New York Times* (14 January 2009). See also Thomas L. Friedman, "War, Timeout, War, Time . . . ," *New York Times* (25 June 2010).

43. Yair Evron, "Deterrence: The campaign against Hamas," *Strategic Assessment* (February 2009), p. 81; International Crisis Group, *Gaza's Unfinished Business*, p. 19n198.

44. International Crisis Group, *Gaza's Unfinished Business*, pp. 7–8.

45. Gideon Levy, "The IDF Has No Mercy for the Children in Gaza Nursery Schools," *Haaretz* (15 January 2009).

46. "Memorandum for the Record" (17 November 1968), n. 13, *Foreign Relations of the United States, 1964–1968*. The quoted phrase is from key US presidential aide Walt W. Rostow.

47. International Crisis Group, *Gaza's Unfinished Business*, p. 19.

48. Noam Chomsky, *The Fateful Triangle: The United States, Israel and the Palestinians* (Boston: 1983), Chapter 3; Norman G. Finkelstein, *Beyond Chutzpah: On the misuse of anti-Semitism and the abuse of history* (Berkeley: 2005; expanded paperback edition, 2008), pp. 337–41. For in-depth analysis, see Finkelstein, *Knowing Too Much*, Chapter 9 ("Israel versus the World").

49. Finkelstein, *"This Time,"* pp. 40–44.

50. Finkelstein, *Knowing Too Much*, Chapter 9.

51. Paul Scham and Osama Abu-Irshaid, *Hamas: Ideological rigidity and political flexibility*, United States Institute of Peace Special Report (Washington, DC: June 2009), pp. 2–4. See also Khaled Hroub, "A 'New Hamas' through Its New Documents," *Journal of Palestine Studies* (Summer 2006), Jeroen Gunning, *Hamas in Politics: Democracy, religion, violence* (New York: 2008), pp. 205–6, 236–37, Jerome Slater, "A Perfect Moral Catastrophe: Just War philosophy and the Israeli attack on Gaza," *Tikkun*, March–April 2009 (a longer and fully footnoted version of this article is posted on www.Tikkun.com), subsection headed "A political settlement with Hamas?," and Henry Siegman, "US Hamas Policy Blocks Middle East Peace," *Noref Report* (September 2010). Hamas's political evolution retraced the PLO's, in which the call for a state in the whole of Palestine was superseded by a "phased" liberation of Palestine, starting with a state in the West Bank and Gaza, and finally acquiescence in a two-state settlement (Shaul Mishal and Avraham

Sela, *The Palestinian Hamas: Vision, violence, and coexistence* (New York: 2006), pp. 108–10).

52. Mouin Rabbani, "A Hamas Perspective on the Movement's Evolving Role: An interview with Khalid Mishal, Part II," *Journal of Palestine Studies* (Summer 2008).

53. Gianni Perrelli, "Con Israele non sarà mai pace" (Interview with Khalid Mishal), *L'espresso* (26 February 2009; http://tinyurl.com/clcw8q).

54. Jimmy Carter, *We Can Have Peace in the Holy Land: A plan that will work* (New York: 2009), pp. 137, 177. See also Nidal al-Mughrabi, "Hamas Would Honor Referendum on Peace with Israel," *Reuters* (1 December 2010).

55. Khaled Hroub, *Hamas: Political thought and practice* (Washington, DC: 2000), p. 44 (see also ibid., p. 254); Sherifa Zuhur, *Hamas and Israel: Conflicting strategies of group-based politics* (Carlisle, PA: 2008), pp. 29–31 (this study was published by the Strategic Studies Institute of the US Army War College). See also Gunning, *Hamas in Politics*, pp. 19–20.

56. "What Hamas Wants," *Mideast Mirror* (22 December 2008).

57. Zuhur, *Hamas and Israel*, pp. ix, 14.

58. Intelligence and Terrorism Information Center at the Israel Intelligence Heritage and Commemoration Center, *The Six Months of the Lull Arrangement* (December 2008), pp. 2, 6, 7. See also point (3) of "Defense Minister Barak's Discussions . . . " (29 August 2008), *WikiLeaks*. According to Egyptians who brokered the June 2008 cease-fire, it provided for an immediate cessation of armed hostilities; a gradual lifting of the economic blockade that, after ten days, would allow for the passage of all products, except materials used in the manufacture of projectiles and explosives; and negotiations after three weeks for a prisoner exchange and the opening of Rafah crossing (see International Crisis Group, *Ending the War in Gaza*, p. 3; Carter, *We Can Have Peace*, pp. 137–38). Af-

ter the abortive coup against Hamas in June 2007, Israel severely restricted entry of goods "not considered essential for
the basic subsistence of the population." It allowed passage
of only a "humanitarian minimum"—a benchmark that was
arbitrarily determined, not sanctioned by international law,
and in fact fell below Gaza's minimal humanitarian needs.
When the June 2008 cease-fire went into effect, Israel per-
mitted only a "slightly increased" movement of supplies
into Gaza. Gisha (Legal Center for Freedom of Movement),
Red Lines Crossed: Destruction of Gaza's infrastructure (August
2009), pp. 11, 13, 41–42, 45–46, 50; see also Gisha, "Israel
Reveals Documents Related to the Gaza Closure Policy"
(21 October 2010).

59. Richard N. Haass and Martin Indyk, "Beyond Iraq: A new
US strategy for the Middle East," and Walter Russell Mead,
"Change They Can Believe In: To make Israel safe, give Pales-
tinians their due," in *Foreign Affairs* (January–February 2009).

60. Mishal and Sela, *Palestinian Hamas*, p. 14.

61. Chomsky, *Fateful Triangle*, Chapters 3 and 5.

62. Yehuda Lukacs, ed., *The Israeli-Palestinian Conflict: A documen-
tary record, 1967–1990* (Cambridge: 1992), pp. 477–79.

63. Yehoshaphat Harkabi, *Israel's Fateful Hour* (New York: 1988),
p. 101.

64. Avner Yaniv, *Dilemmas of Security: Politics, strategy and the
Israeli experience in Lebanon* (Oxford: 1987), pp. 20–23, 50–54,
67–70, 87–89, 100–1, 105–6, 113, 143, 294n46. Robert Fisk, *Pity
the Nation: The abduction of Lebanon* (New York: 1990), pp. 197,
232.

65. Saed Bannoura, "Livni Calls for a Large-Scale Military Offensive in Gaza," IMEMC & Agencies (10 December 2008; http://
tinyurl.com/chqtk7).

66. Uri Blau, "IDF Sources: Conditions not yet optimal for Gaza
exit," *Haaretz* (8 January 2009); Barak Ravid, "Disinformation,

Secrecy, and Lies: How the Gaza offensive came about," *Haaretz* (28 December 2008).

67. Nancy Kanwisher, Johannes Haushofer, and Anat Biletzki, "Reigniting Violence: How do cease-fires end?," *Huffington Post* (6 January 2009; http://tinyurl.com/dfujv3). See also Johannes Haushofer, Anat Biletzki, and Nancy Kanwisher, "Both Sides Retaliate in the Israeli-Palestinian Conflict," *Proceedings of the National Academy of Sciences of the United States* (4 October 2010).

68. Slater, "A Perfect Moral Catastrophe" (subsection headed "A cease-fire").

69. Zvi Bar'el, "Crushing the Tahadiyeh," *Haaretz* (16 November 2008); Uri Avnery, "The Calculations behind Israel's Slaughter of Palestinians in Gaza," *redress.cc* (2 January 2009; http://tinyurl.com/a6pzlx).

70. Amnesty International annual report 2009 entry for *Israel and the Occupied Palestinian Territories*; see also Human Rights Watch, *Rockets from Gaza: Harm to civilians from Palestinian armed groups' rocket attacks* (New York: August 2009), p. 2.

71. Intelligence and Terrorism Information Center, *Six Months*, p. 3.

72. "Hamas Wants Better Terms for Truce," *Jerusalem Post* (21 December 2008); Bradley Burston, "Can the First Gaza War Be Stopped before It Starts?," *Haaretz* (22 December 2008). Diskin told the Israeli cabinet that Hamas would renew the truce if Israel lifted the siege of Gaza, stopped military attacks, and extended the truce to the West Bank.

73. "Gaza Residents 'Terribly Trapped,'" *BBC News* (4 November 2008; www.bbc.co.uk).

74. Gisha, *Red Lines*, pp. 5, 26, 33.

75. Sara Roy, "If Gaza Falls . . . ," *London Review of Books* (1 January 2009).

76. International Crisis Group, *Ending the War in Gaza*, pp. 3, 10–11.

77. Burston, "Can the First Gaza War."
78. Khalid Mishal, "This Brutality Will Never Break Our Will to Be Free," *Guardian* (6 January 2009).
79. It was not the first time Israel sought to provoke Hamas after it mooted a modus vivendi. Two Israeli academic authorities on Hamas recalled that in September 1997, just days before an abortive Israeli assassination attempt on Khalid Mishal, "Jordan's King Hussein delivered a message from the Hamas leadership to Israel's Prime Minister Benjamin Netanyahu. In it Hamas suggested opening an indirect dialogue with the Israeli government, to be mediated by the king, toward achieving a cessation of violence, as well as a 'discussion of all matters.' But the message was ignored or missed and, in any case, became irrelevant following the attempt" on the Hamas leader's life (Mishal and Sela, *Palestinian Hamas*, p. 72; see also McGeough, *Kill Khalid*, esp. pp. 141, 146, 226).

2/ PUNISH, HUMILIATE AND TERRORIZE

1. *Report of the United Nations Fact-Finding Mission on the Gaza Conflict* (25 September 2009), paras. 1, 151. Hereafter: Goldstone Report.
2. Ibid., paras. 144, 162; Bill Moyers, *Journal* (23 October 2009; http://tinyurl.com/yllft94). For the extended correspondence between Goldstone and the Government of Israel, see Goldstone Report, Annex II, pp. 434–50; see also Israel Ministry of Foreign Affairs website, "The Goldstone Mission—FAQ" (http://tinyurl.com/yjvunox).
3. For a critical but ultimately positive assessment of the Report by "recognized experts" in the relevant bodies of international law, see *Report of an Expert Meeting which Assessed Procedural Criticisms Made of the UN Fact-Finding Mission on the Gaza Conflict (The Goldstone Report)* (London: 27 November 2009).
4. Goldstone Report, paras. 63, 1213–14.

5. Ibid., paras. 1215, 1892.
6. Ibid., paras. 1208, 1884.
7. Ibid., para. 1893.
8. Ibid., para. 1898. Goldstone afterwards recalled that, although initially fearful of traveling to Gaza—"I had nightmares about being kidnapped. You know, it was very difficult, especially for a Jew, to go into an area controlled by Hamas"—he was "struck by the warmth of the people that we met and who we dealt with in Gaza" (Moyers, *Journal*).
9. Goldstone Report, paras. 46, 50, 60, 937, 961, 987, 1006, 1171–75, 1935.
10. Ibid., paras. 75, 1334–35, 1936. The fact-finding committee chaired by Goldstone's distinguished South African colleague John Dugard went somewhat further. It concluded that, during Israel's "heinous and inhuman" attack, it was culpable for war crimes, such as "indiscriminate and disproportionate attacks on civilians," "killing, wounding and terrorizing civilians," "wanton destruction of property," and the bombing and shelling of hospitals and ambulances and obstructing the evacuation of the wounded. It further found that Israel was guilty of crimes against humanity, including the intentional and "reckless" killing of civilians, "mass killings—'extermination'—in certain cases," and "persecution." It did not, however, hold Israel culpable for the crime of genocide: "the main reason for the operation was not to destroy a group, as required for the crime of genocide, but to engage in a vicious exercise of collective punishment designed either to compel the population to reject Hamas as the governing authority of Gaza or to subdue the population into a state of submission." Still, it found that "individual soldiers may well have had such an intent [i.e., to commit genocide] and might therefore be prosecuted for this crime." *Report of the Independent Fact-Finding Committee on Gaza: No safe place.* Presented to the League of

Arab States (30 April 2009), paras. 20, 22–23, 25–30 of Executive Summary; paras. 405, 485–91, 496–98, 500–4, 506–10, 519–20, 526–29, 540–47, 554–58, 572–73. Hereafter: Dugard Report.

11. Goldstone Report, para. 1895.

12. Ibid., paras. 108, 1691, 1953. The Dugard Committee held Hamas and other militant Palestinian groups culpable for war crimes, such as "indiscriminate and disproportionate attacks on civilians" and "killing, wounding and terrorizing civilians," although it entered the caveat that "there are a number of factors that reduce their moral blameworthiness but not their criminal responsibility"; among them, "Palestinians have been denied their right to self-determination by Israel and have long been subjected to a cruel siege by Israel," "the scale of Israel's action," and "the great difference in both the weapons capability of the opposing sides and the use of their respective weaponry" (Dugard Report, paras. 21, 24, 35 of Executive Summary; paras. 457, 484, 495, 499, 575–77).

13. Dinah PoKempner, general counsel of Human Rights Watch, noted that it was "hardly surprising" that the space devoted to Hamas was "fairly brief because there is little factual dispute about whether the Gaza authorities tolerated firing of rockets onto Israel's civilian areas, and no legal ambiguity to discuss" ("Valuing the Goldstone Report," *Global Governance* 16 (2010), p. 153).

14. Moyers, *Journal*.

15. "Hungry Like the Wolfowitz," *Georgetown Voice* (6 November 2003).

16. "What Women Should Do in a Difficult Situation" (4 September 1932), in *The Collected Works of Mahatma Gandhi* (Ahmedabad), vol. 51, pp. 18–19, "Discussion with Mahadev Desai" (4 September 1932), in ibid., vol. 51, pp. 24–25, "Discussion with B. G. Kher and Others" (15 August 1940), in ibid., vol. 72, p. 388,

"Discussion with Bharatanand" (2 September 1940), in ibid., vol. 72, p. 434, "Message to States' People" (1 October 1941), in ibid., vol. 74, p. 368, "Speech at Prayer Meeting" (5 November 1947), in ibid., vol. 89, p. 481.

17. "Speech at Goalundo" (6 November 1946), in ibid., vol. 86, p. 86.

18. See Chapter 1 above.

19. Goldstone Report, para. 205.

20. The Report makes passing mention in this context of "the right of return for refugees" (ibid., paras. 92, 1509).

21. Ibid., paras. 206–7.

22. Ibid., para. 1440.

23. Ibid., para. 1503.

24. Ibid., paras. 1504–5.

25. Ibid., paras. 1535–37. The Mission explicitly stated that it "considers East Jerusalem part of the Occupied Palestinian Territories" (ibid., p. 369n1062).

26. Ibid., para. 1546.

27. Ibid., para. 1946.

28. Ibid., para. 1947.

29. Ibid., para. 1876.

30. Ibid., paras. 127, 1857, 1975.

31. Ibid., para. 1969.

32. Ibid., paras. 128, 1873, 1971(b).

33. Ibid., paras. 1971–74. The Report explicitly called on Israel to "release Palestinians who are detained in Israeli prisons in connection with the occupation."

34. Amira Hass, "The One Thing Worse Than Denying the Gaza Report," *Haaretz* (17 September 2009), Gideon Levy, "Disgrace in the Hague," *Haaretz* (17 September 2009), Gideon Levy, "Goldstone's Gaza Probe Did Israel a Favor," *Haaretz* (1 October 2009), Yitzhak Laor, "The National Choir," *Haaretz* (22 September 2009), Yitzhak Laor, "Turning Off the

Lights," *Haaretz* (7 October 2009), Zeev Sternhell, "A Permanent Moral Stain," *Haaretz* (25 September 2009), Larry Derfner, "A Wake-up Call from Judge Goldstone," *Jerusalem Post* (16 September 2009), Larry Derfner, "Our Exclusive Right to Self-Defense," *Jerusalem Post* (7 October 2009), Larry Derfner, "Some Victims We Are," *Jerusalem Post* (28 October 2009). Both the head of the dovish Meretz party and *Haaretz* editorials called on the Israeli government to set up a commission of inquiry. Gil Hoffman and Haviv Rettig Gur, "Oron Calls for Israeli Cast Lead Probe," *Jerusalem Post* (18 September 2009), "A Committee of Inquiry is Needed," *Haaretz* (18 September 2009), "Only an External Probe Will Do," *Haaretz* (3 October 2009), "Israel's Whitewash," *Haaretz* (28 January 2010).

35. "Statement by President Shimon Peres: 'Goldstone Mission Report is a mockery of history,'" *mfa.gov.il* (16 September 2009; http://tinyurl.com/y9yxzpa); Shuki Sadeh, "Peres: Goldstone is a small man out to hurt Israel," *Haaretz* (12 November 2009).

36. Barak Ravid and Natasha Mozgovaya, "Netanyahu Calls UN Gaza Probe a 'Kangaroo Court' against Israel," *Haaretz* (16 September 2009).

37. "Rights Council to Debate Gaza War," *Aljazeera.net* (15 October 2009; http://tinyurl.com/ykfjth3); Barak Ravid, "Israel Slams Goldstone 'Misrepresentations' of Internal Probes into Gaza War," *Haaretz* (7 February 2010).

38. Barak Ravid, "Israel Prepares to Fight War Crimes Trials after Goldstone Gaza Report," *Haaretz* (20 October 2009); Barak Ravid, "Israel to Set Up Team to Review Gaza War Probe," *Haaretz* (26 October 2009). Zeev Sternhell, "With a Conscience That Is Always Clear," *Haaretz* (30 October 2009). Reacting to Netanyahu's proposal, Goldstone observed that "It seems to me to contain an implicit acceptance that they broke

the law that now is, and that's why it needs to be changed" (Moyers, *Journal*).

39. Rebecca Anna Stoil and Tovah Lazaroff, "EU to Debate Goldstone Report," *Jerusalem Post* (24 February 2010).

40. "Dershowitz: Goldstone is a traitor," *Jerusalem Post* (31 January 2010).

41. Hoffman and Gur, "Oron Calls"; Donald MacIntyre, "Israelis Hit Back at UN Report Alleging War Crimes in Gaza," *Independent* (17 September 2009); Ravid and Mozgovaya, "Netanyahu Calls."

42. Michael Oren, "UN Report a Victory for Terror," *Boston Globe* (24 September 2009); Michael Oren, "Address to AJC" (28 April 2010; http://tinyurl.com/37xngbo); Michael B. Oren, "Deep Denial: Why the Holocaust still matters," *New Republic* (6 October 2009). For critical analysis of Oren's scholarship, see Norman G. Finkelstein, *Knowing Too Much: Why the American Jewish romance with Israel is coming to an end* (New York: 2012), pp. 161–81.

43. Israel Harel, "Venom and Destruction," *Haaretz* (18 September 2009); Israel Harel, "Don't Establish an Investigative Panel," *Haaretz* (1 October 2009); Jack Khoury, "Goldstone Tells Obama: Show me flaws in Gaza report," *Haaretz* (22 October 2009).

44. Stephen Roth Institute for the Study of Contemporary Antisemitism and Racism, *Antisemitism Worldwide 2009* (2010; www.tau.ac.il/Anti-Semitism/), pp. 29, 37, 39.

45. "Israel's Jewish Public: Goldstone report biased against IDF," *ynetnews.com* (18 October 2009; http://tinyurl.com/yh36quh).

46. Yehezkel Dror, "Why Israel Should Have Cooperated with Goldstone on Gaza," *Haaretz* (21 September 2009).

47. Uri Avnery, "UM-Shmum, UM-Boom," *Gush Shalom* (19 September 2009; http://tinyurl.com/m32fwl).

48. "Wiesel: If Ahmadinejad were assassinated, I wouldn't shed a tear," *Haaretz* (9 February 2010), "I Wouldn't Cry If He Was Killed," *Jerusalem Post* (9 February 2010).

49. Alan M. Dershowitz, "Goldstone Investigation Undercuts Human Rights," *Jerusalem Post* blog ("Double Standard Watch") (17 September 2009; http://tinyurl.com/m27byk); Alan Dershowitz, "Goldstone Criticizes UN Council on Human Rights," *Huffington Post* (22 October 2009; http://tinyurl.com/yjqmx4s); Alan M. Dershowitz, "Goldstone Backs Away from Report: The two faces of an international poseur," *Jerusalem Post* blog ("Double Standard Watch") (15 October 2009; http://tinyurl.com/yhqec6o); "Dershowitz: Goldstone is a traitor," *Jerusalem Post*; Josh Nathan-Kazis, "Dershowitz Explains Critical Goldstone Remark," *Forward* (3 February 2010); Tehiya Barak, "Judge Goldstone's Dark Past," *ynetnews.com* (6 May 2010; http://tinyurl.com/27h4nde).

50. Alan Dershowitz, *The Case against the Goldstone Report: A study in evidentiary bias* (www.alandershowitz.com/goldstone.pdf).

51. Bernard-Henri Lévy, "It's Time to Stop Demonizing Israel," *Haaretz* (8 June 2010). Joshua Muravchik, "Goldstone: An exegesis," *World Affairs* (May/June 2010). Muravchik also made the astonishing claim that Goldstone never asked witnesses to Israeli attacks "whether a Palestinian gunman was nearby." In fact, every account of an Israeli attack in the Goldstone Report includes testimony bearing on the presence of Palestinian fighters in the vicinity. See also Jeffrey Goldberg, "J Street, Down the Rabbit Hole," *Atlantic* blog (30 September 2010), falsely alleging that "Goldstone's work [was] heavily reliant on Hamas for uncorroborated information."

52. Moyers, *Journal*.

53. Eric Fingerhut, "AIPAC Condemns Goldstone Report," *Jewish Telegraphic Agency* (17 September 2009; http://tinyurl.com/y8rkgwo).

54. American Jewish Committee, "Letter to Secretary Clinton Urges Condemnation of Goldstone Report" (23 September 2009; http://tinyurl.com/ya4bqqz).

55. "Rice: 'Serious concerns' about the Goldstone Report," *Jewish Telegraphic Agency* (17 September 2009; http://tinyurl.com/yakxdlv).

56. House Subcommittee on the Middle East and South Asia, "Ackerman Blasts Goldstone Report as 'Pompous, Tendentious, One-sided Political Diatribe'" (16 September 2009; http://tinyurl.com/yhs9ckd).

57. "H. RES. 867, 111th Congress" (23 October 2009; http://tinyurl.com/yhu3c7e); Natasha Mozgovaya and Barak Ravid, "US House Backs Resolution to Condemn Goldstone Gaza Report," *Haaretz* (5 November 2009); Nima Shirazi, "Goldstone-walled! US Congress endorses Israeli war crimes," *MRzine* (12 November 2009; http://tinyurl.com/y8kenjd).

58. "Goldstone Sends Letter to Berman, Ros-Lehtinen Correcting Factual Errors in HR 867, Which Opposes UN Fact-Finding Report on Gaza," *uruknet.info* (29 October 2009; http://tinyurl.com/y8kvt5m). After Goldstone submitted his rebuttal, one of the resolution's sponsors entered some cosmetic revisions in it. Spencer Ackerman, "Berman Puts New Language into Anti-Goldstone Resolution," *washingtonindependent.com* (3 November 2009; http://tinyurl.com/yaonaa6). J Street called for a "better, balanced resolution" than the House draft, but one that still would "urge the United States to make clear that it will use its veto to prevent any referral of this matter to the International Criminal Court." "J Street Position on H.Res. 867" (30 October 2009; http://tinyurl.com/yd8u4za).

59. Nathan Guttman, "Israel, US Working to Limit Damage of Goldstone Report," *Haaretz* (27 September 2009).

60. US Department of State, *2009 Human Rights Report* (http://tinyurl.com/yhddnjt).

61. Khoury, "Goldstone Tells Obama"; "Goldstone Dares US on Gaza Report," *Aljazeera.net* (22 October 2009; http://tinyurl

.com/yg6zafm); Human Rights Watch, "UN: US, EU Undermine Justice for Gaza Conflict" (1 October 2009).

62. An administration official initially stated in private that the US would block UN action on the report, but the White House subsequently repudiated the statement. "US Pledges to Quash Goldstone Recommendations," *Jewish Telegraphic Agency* (22 September 2009); "White House: Official 'misspoke' on Goldstone report," *Jewish Telegraphic Agency* (23 September 2009); Amos Harel and Avi Issacharoff, "Israel Demands PA Drop War Crimes Suit at The Hague," *Haaretz* (27 September 2009).

63. Howard Schneider and Colum Mynch, "UN Panel Defers Vote on Gaza Report," *Washington Post* (3 October 2009), Amira Hass, "PA Move to Thwart Goldstone Gaza Report Shocks Palestinian Public," *Haaretz* (4 October 2009).

64. "The Human Rights Situation in the Occupied Palestinian Territory, Including East Jerusalem" (A/HRC/RES/S-12/1) (16 October 2009). It was gleefully reported by many of Goldstone's critics that he disapproved of the resolution. The allegation was a half truth and a whole lie: Goldstone disapproved of the first draft but it was modified after he expressed reservations and he approved of the final version that was voted on (Moyers, *Journal*).

65. United Nations General Assembly, "Follow-up to the Report of the United Nations Fact-Finding Mission on the Gaza Conflict" (A/64/L.11) (2 November 2009). Shlomo Shamir, "UN General Assembly Adopts Goldstone Report," *Haaretz* (6 November 2009).

66. Shlomo Shamir, "Israel: UN 'detached from reality' for adopting Goldstone report," *Haaretz* (6 November 2009).

67. United Nations General Assembly, *Follow-up to the Report of the United Nations Fact-Finding Mission on the Gaza Conflict: Report of the Secretary-General* (A/64/651; 4 February 2010).

68. United Nations General Assembly, "Follow-up to the Report of the United Nations Fact-Finding Mission on the Gaza Conflict

(II)" (A/64/L.48; 23 February 2010). The low vote count was probably due to a snowstorm that day.

69. "European Parliament Resolution of 10 March 2010 on Implementation of the Goldstone Recommendations on Israel/ Palestine" (P7_TA-PROV(2010)0054); Leigh Phillips, "Despite Heavy Lobbying, EU Parliament Endorses Goldstone Report," *euobserver.com* (10 March 2010; http://euobserver .com/9/29650); "EU Parliament Backs Goldstone Report," *Jerusalem Post* (10 March 2010).

70. State of Israel, *Gaza Operation Investigations: An update* (January 2010); State of Israel, *Gaza Operation Investigations: Second update* (July 2010). For critical analysis of Israel's original July 2009 report, *The Operation in Gaza, 27 December 2008–18 January 2009: Factual and legal aspects*, see Norman G. Finkelstein, *"This Time We Went Too Far": Truth and consequences of the Gaza invasion*, revised and expanded paperback edition (New York: 2011), Chapters 3 and 4.

71. *Gaza Operation Investigations: An update*, paras. 100, 108, 137; *Gaza Operation Investigations: Second update*, paras. 10, 11, 37, 46, 60, 73, 74, 94, 102.

72. Amos Harel, "MESS Report: Gaza war probes are changing Israel's defiant ways," *Haaretz* (22 July 2010).

73. *Gaza Operation Investigations: Second update*, para. 105.

74. Ibid., paras. 150–56.

75. After the initial update, *Haaretz* editorialized that the Israeli investigations were "not persuasive that enough has been done to reach the truth," but in a subsequent editorial *Haaretz* validated the second round of investigations and implied that it was time to close the book on the Goldstone Report. "Israel Is Being Evasive Again," *Haaretz* (1 February 2010); "Thanks to the Critics," *Haaretz* (27 July 2010). Both Amnesty International and Human Rights Watch wholly dismissed the first round of investigations, while HRW stated after

the second update that, although "some results" had been achieved, the Israeli investigations still "fall far short of addressing the widespread and serious allegations of unlawful conduct during the fighting." Amnesty International, "Latest Israeli Response to Gaza Investigations Totally Inadequate" (2 February 2010); Human Rights Watch, "Military Investigations Fail Gaza War Victims" (7 February 2010); Human Rights Watch, "Wartime Inquiries Fall Short" (10 August 2010).

76. UN News Service, "UN Rights Chief Unveils Members of Independent Probe into Gaza Conflict" (14 June 2010).

77. *Report of the Committee of Independent Experts in International Humanitarian and Human Rights Laws to Monitor and Assess Any Domestic, Legal or Other Proceedings Undertaken by Both the Government of Israel and the Palestinian Side, in the Light of General Assembly Resolution 64/254, Including the Independence, Effectiveness, Genuineness of These Investigations and Their Conformity with International Standards* (21 September 2010). The Israel lobby defamed the eminent German jurist who chaired the committee, eventually forcing his resignation. Benjamin Weinthal and Jonny Paul, "Dershowitz: Goldstone follow-up commission head a 'bigot,'" *Jerusalem Post* (2 November 2010); Benjamin Weinthal, "Tomuschat, Head of Goldstone Follow-up Committee, Resigns," *Jerusalem Post* (3 December 2010).

78. *Report of the Committee,* paras. 42, 55.

79. Ibid., para. 101.

80. Ibid., paras. 40, 83. The committee reported that Israel convicted one soldier for the crime of looting, while a Hamas submission gave "examples of criminal proceedings . . . , including a case where a number of defendants were convicted and imprisoned."

81. Amnesty International, "Time for International Justice Solution for Gaza Conflict Victims" (23 September 2010).

82. Hoffman and Gur, "Oron Calls"; Eitan Haber, "In Wake of Goldstone Report, Israel Must Launch Battle for Its Image," *ynetnews.com* (17 September 2009; http://tinyurl.com/y85me4a).

83. Richard Falk, "The Goldstone Report: Ordinary text, extraordinary event," *Global Governance* 16 (2010), p. 173. A member of the Goldstone Mission noted "some 300" human rights investigations into Cast Lead, which were "remarkable in the unanimity of their findings against the IDF actions" (Desmond Travers, "Operation Cast Lead: Legal and doctrinal asymmetries in a military operation," *An Cosantóir*, Irish Defense Forces Review (2010), p. 103). Some critics alleged that the Goldstone Report was more "vicious" than the human rights reports that preceded it (see Ethan Bronner, "Israel Poised to Challenge a UN Report on Gaza," *New York Times*, 23 January 2010), but the contention lacked credibility. In fact, the Goldstone Report was in crucial respects the most cautious and conservative of the human rights reports on Gaza: whereas HRW explicitly denoted Israel's use of white phosphorus in civilian areas a "war crime" (see Finkelstein, *"This Time,"* pp. 81–82), the Goldstone Report did not; whereas the Dugard Report concluded that "individual soldiers" might have been guilty of genocide, the Goldstone Report did not; and whereas Amnesty recommended a comprehensive arms embargo on Israel (and Hamas) (see Finkelstein, *"This Time,"* pp. 98–99), the Goldstone Report did not.

84. Moyers, *Journal*; "Will Goldstone's Gaza Report Prove Him Just a Naive Idealist?," *Haaretz* (23 September 2009); "'My Father is a Zionist, Loves Israel,'" *Jerusalem Post* (16 September 2009); "Goldstone's Daughter: My father's participation softened UN Gaza report," *Haaretz* (16 September 2009); "Tikkun Interview with Judge Richard Goldstone" (1 October 2009; http://tinyurl.com/yhg3cfk).

85. Anshel Pfeffer, "Goldstone: Holocaust shaped view on war crimes," *Haaretz* (18 September 2009).

86. Amir Mizroch, "Analysis: Grappling with Goldstone," *Jerusalem Post* (18 September 2009); Amir Mizroch, "What South African Jews Think of Richard Goldstone," *Jerusalem Post* (1 October 2009); R. W. Johnson, "Who is Richard Goldstone?," *Radio Free Europe/Radio Liberty* (20 October 2009; http://tinyurl.com/yha38ed); Ashley Rindsberg, "UN's Goldstone Sent 13-Year-Old Boy to Prison for Protesting Apartheid," *Huffington Post* (19 November 2009; http://tinyurl.com/yefdang); Dershowitz, "Goldstone Investigation." It must nonetheless be said that, in interviews and statements after the report was published, Goldstone seemingly backpedaled from its more damning conclusions and downplayed the extent of Israeli crimes; see, e.g., Richard Goldstone, "Justice in Gaza," *New York Times* (17 September 2009), Richard Goldstone, "Who's Being Unfair?," *Jerusalem Post* (21 September 2009), Gal Beckerman, "Goldstone: 'If this was a court of law, there would have been nothing proven,'" *Forward* (16 October 2009), "Tikkun Interview with Judge Richard Goldstone."

87. Harold Evans, "A Moral Atrocity," *Guardian* (20 October 2009).

88. Moyers, *Journal.*

89. Aluf Benn, "In Wake of UN Gaza Probe, How Can Israel Go to War Again?," *Haaretz* (16 September 2009); Ari Shavit, "Watch Out for the Goldstoners," *Haaretz* (8 October 2009). See also Gideon Levy, "Peres, Not Goldstone, Is the Small Man," *Haaretz* (15 November 2009), and The Reut Institute, *Building a Political Firewall against Israel's Delegitimization* (Tel Aviv: March 2010), paras. 40,106.

90. "PM: Israel faces the 'Goldstone threat,'" *Jerusalem Post* (23 December 2009).

91. Barak Ravid and Anshel Pfeffer, "Israel Seeks Obama Backing on Gaza Probe," *Haaretz* (26 September 2009).

92. Yotam Feldman, "ICC May Try IDF Officer in Wake of Gold-stone Gaza Report," *Haaretz* (24 September 2009); Raphael Ahren, "Israeli Soldiers from South Africa Feel Heat of Prosecution Drive in Old Country," *Haaretz* (22 November 2009).

93. Livni reportedly cancels UK visit, fearing arrest," *Haaretz* (16 December 2009); Danna Harman, "Belgian Lawyers to Charge Barak and Livni for War Crimes," *Haaretz* (23 June 2010).

94. Assaf Gefen, "Are We Hiding Something?," *ynetnews.com* (8 February 2010; http://tinyurl.com/34zuvux).

3/ WE KNOW A LOT MORE TODAY

1. Richard Goldstone, "Reconsidering the Goldstone Report on Israel and War Crimes," *Washington Post* (1 April 2011).

2. *Report of the United Nations Fact-Finding Mission on the Gaza Conflict* (25 September 2009). See Chapter 2 above.

3. Barak Ravid, "Netanyahu to UN: Retract Gaza war report in wake of Goldstone's comments," *Haaretz* (2 April 2011); "Lieberman Praises Goldstone for 'Vindicating' Israel," *Jerusalem Post* (2 April 2011).

4. US Agrees: Israel did not commit Cast Lead war crimes," *Jerusalem Post* (5 April 2011); Natasha Mozgovaya, "US Senate Urges UN to Rescind Goldstone's Gaza Report," *Haaretz* (15 April 2011).

5. Donald Macintyre, "Israeli Commander: 'We rewrote the rules of war for Gaza,'" *Independent* (3 February 2010); Anshel Pfeffer, "IDF Officer: Gaza civilians risked to protect Israel troops during war," *Haaretz* (3 February 2010).

6. Human Rights Watch, *"I Lost Everything": Israel's unlawful destruction of property during Operation Cast Lead* (New York: 2010).

7. Intelligence and Terrorism Information Center, *Hamas and the Terrorist Threat from the Gaza Strip: The main findings of the Goldstone Report versus the factual findings* (March 2010), pp. 3, 35; 95, 97; VIII, 57; 120; 315, 321–22.

8. Kim Sengupta and Donald Macintyre, "Israeli Cabinet Divided over Fresh Gaza Surge," *Independent* (13 January 2009); Public Committee Against Torture in Israel (PCATI), *No Second Thoughts: The changes in the Israeli Defense Forces' combat doctrine in light of "Operation Cast Lead"* (Jerusalem: November 2009), p. 28.

9. International Crisis Group, *Ending the War in Gaza* (5 January 2009), p. 19; International Crisis Group, *Gaza's Unfinished Business* (April 2009), p. 19.

10. Guy Bechor, "Israel Is Back," *ynetnews.com* (19 February 2010).

11. International Court of Justice, *Advisory Opinion on the Legality of the Threat or Use of Nuclear Weapons* (1996), "Dissenting Opinion of Judge Weeramantry," Chapter III, "Humanitarian Law," section 10, "Specific rules of the humanitarian laws," (a) "The prohibition against causing unnecessary suffering" (emphasis in original).

12. Yoram Dinstein, *Conduct of Hostilities under the Law of International Armed Conflict* (Cambridge: 2004), p. 117.

13. "Judge Goldstone's Notes for the Panel on Civilians in War Zones," paras. 29–35 (maurice-ostroff.tripod.com/id315 .html).

14. Amnesty International, *Amnesty International's Updated Assessment of Israeli and Palestinian Investigations into the Gaza Conflict* (18 March 2011).

15. *Report of the Committee of Independent Experts in International Humanitarian and Human Rights Law Established Pursuant to Council Resolution 13/9* (18 March 2011).

16. Amnesty International, *Amnesty International's Updated Assessment*; B'Tselem (Israeli Information Center for Human Rights in the Occupied Territories), "Goldstone Then and Now" (5 April 2011).

17. Amnesty International, *Amnesty International's Updated Assessment*.

18. UN Office for the Coordination of Humanitarian Affairs, *Protection of Civilians Weekly Report* (1–8 January 2009); Amnesty International, *Operation "Cast Lead": 22 Days of death and destruction* (2009), p. 20.

19. Amira Hass, "What Led to IDF Bombing House Full of Civilians during Gaza War?," *Haaretz* (24 October 2010).

20. State of Israel, *Gaza Operation Investigations: An update* (January 2010), pp. 41–44. Although critical evidence belied the Israeli version of what happened (Anshel Pfeffer, "UN Insists Israel Bombed Flour Mill during Cast Lead," *Haaretz* (4 February 2010); Human Rights Watch, "*I Lost Everything*," pp. 5, 83–86), Israel stuck to its original story (*Gaza Operation Investigations: Second update* (July 2010), paras. 141–45).

21. State of Israel, *Gaza Operation Investigations: Second update*, para. 123.

22. Ibid., para. 68.

23. "Hamas Confirms Losses in Cast Lead for First Time," *Jerusalem Post* (1 November 2010).

24. "Judge Goldstone's Notes," para. 24.

25. Yaakov Lappin, "IDF Releases Cast Lead Casualty Number," *Jerusalem Post* (26 March 2009).

26. Palestinian Center for Human Rights, "Confirmed Figures Reveal the True Extent of the Destruction Inflicted upon the Gaza Strip" (12 March 2009); Al Mezan Center for Human Rights, "Cast Lead Offensive in Numbers" (2 August 2009); "B'Tselem's Investigation of Fatalities in Operation Cast Lead" (9 September 2009).

27. The overall veracity of Israeli figures could be tested on the basis of the "under 16" sub-classification. Whereas Israel alleged that 89 Palestinians under age 16 were killed, B'Tselem reported that 252 Palestinians under 16 were killed and that it "has copies of birth certificates and death certificates along with other documents regarding the vast majority of the

minors who were killed." See also PCATI, *No Second Thoughts*, pp. 9–11. This study showed that Israel abruptly altered the figures it tabulated for Palestinian deaths, and it concluded that "the casualty estimates provided by other sources (around 1,400 killed) are more credible than those provided by the IDF spokesperson."

28. http://tinyurl.com/yhddnjt.

29. Human Rights Watch, "*I Lost Everything*," p. 7.

30. Human Rights Watch, *Rain of Fire: Israel's unlawful use of white phosphorus in Gaza* (New York: March 2009).

31. "UK Officer Slams 'Pavlovian' Criticism of IDF after Gaza War," *Haaretz* (22 February 2010).

32. See Norman G. Finkelstein, *"This Time We Went Too Far": Truth and consequences of the Gaza invasion*, revised and expanded paperback edition (New York: 2011), Chapter 3.

33. In mid-2012, another Israeli soldier, who killed two women waving a white flag, was convicted of "illegal use of weapons" and sentenced to 45 days in prison.

34. B'Tselem (Israeli Information Center for Human Rights in the Occupied Territories), *Void of Responsibility: Israel military policy not to investigate killings of Palestinians by soldiers* (Jerusalem: September 2010); Yesh Din, *Exceptions: Prosecution of IDF soldiers during and after the second intifada* (Tel Aviv: September 2008). For official Israeli claims intended to boost the credibility of its investigations, see Finkelstein, *"This Time,"* p. 282n79.

35. See Chapter 2 above.

36. "Dershowitz: Goldstone follow-up commission head a 'bigot,'" *Jerusalem Post* (2 November 2010); Benjamin Weinthal, "Tomuschat, Head of Goldstone Follow-up Committee, Resigns," *Jerusalem Post* (3 December 2010). Tomuschat was replaced by Judge Mary McGowan Davis of the New York State Supreme Court. Although she wasn't a pushover, her

follow-up report still bent over backwards for Israel. For example, it gives guarded praise to the preposterous Turkel Report that exonerated Israel of any wrongdoing in its assault on the Gaza Freedom Flotilla (*Report of the Committee of Independent Experts*, para. 39). For a detailed analysis of the Turkel Report, see Finkelstein, *"This Time,"* Appendix 2; see also Chapter 4 below.

37. Ethan Bronner and Jennifer Medina, "Past Holds Clue to Goldstone's Shift on the Gaza War," *New York Times* (19 April 2011).

38. "Thanks to the Critics," *Haaretz* (27 July 2010).

39. "Dershowitz is Not Welcome Here!," *Cape Times* (24 March 2011).

40. Hina Jilani, Christine Chinkin, and Desmond Travers, "Goldstone Report: Statement issued by members of UN mission on Gaza war," *Guardian* (14 April 2011).

41. Roger Cohen, "The Goldstone Chronicles," *New York Times* (7 April 2011); Akiva Eldar, "What Exactly Did Goldstone 'Retract' from His Report on Gaza?," *Haaretz* (12 April 2011).

42. "NY Times: We turned down a different version of Goldstone retraction," *Haaretz* (5 April 2011).

43. *Report of the Independent Fact-Finding Committee on Gaza: No safe place.* Presented to the League of Arab States (30 April 2009), paras. 556, 573. For more on this report, see Finkelstein, *"This Time,"* Chapter 3; see also endnotes to Chapters 1 and 2 above.

44. John Dugard, "Where Now for the Goldstone Report?," *New Statesman* (6 April 2011).

4/ DANGEROUS AND RECKLESS ACT

1. "The Rubble that Was Gaza," *World Food Program News* (25 January 2009; http://tinyurl.com/27xk5cy). See also European Commission, *Damage Assessment and Needs Identification in the Gaza Strip, Final Report* (March 2009), pp. xv, 93.

2. Desmond Travers, "Operation Cast Lead: Legal and doctrinal asymmetries in a military operation," *An Cosantóir*, Irish Defense Forces Review (2010), pp. 103–5.

3. Oxfam, "Gaza Weekly Update" (30 May–5 June 2010); Human Rights Watch, "Israel: Full, impartial investigation of flotilla killings essential" (31 May 2010); World Health Organization, "Medical Supplies Blocked from Entering Gaza" (1 June 2010); International Committee of the Red Cross, "Gaza Closure: Not another year!" (14 June 2010).

4. The most authoritative legal analysis is a document prepared by an investigative mission mandated by the UN Human Rights Council, *Report of the International Fact-Finding Mission to Investigate Violations of International Law, Including International Humanitarian and Human Rights Law, Resulting from the Israeli Attacks on the Flotilla of Ships Carrying Humanitarian Assistance* (27 September 2010). Hereafter: *Report of the Fact-Finding Mission*. The mission was headed up by a retired Judge of the International Criminal Court and included the former Chief Prosecutor of the United Nations-backed Special Court for Sierra Leone. It concluded that "the blockade was inflicting disproportionate damage upon the civilian population in the Gaza Strip and as such the interception could not be justified and therefore has to be considered illegal" (para. 53); "one of the principal motives behind the imposition of the blockade was a desire to punish the people of the Gaza Strip for having elected Hamas. The combination of this motive and the effect of the restrictions on the Gaza Strip leave no doubt that Israel's actions and policies amount to collective punishment as defined by international law" (para. 54).

5. The passengers initially used water hoses to repel the assault, which the International Maritime Organization has "recommended as a means to prevent an attempted boarding by

pirates and armed robbers" (*Report of the Fact-Finding Mission*, p. 25n68).

6. Israeli vilification focused on *Mavi Marmara* passengers belonging to the sponsoring Turkish group IHH (İnsani Yardım Vakfı, or The Foundation for Human Rights and Freedoms and Humanitarian Relief), which was alleged to be a terrorist organization or accused of having close links with terrorist organizations. See Intelligence and Terrorism Information Center, *Conspicuous among the Passengers and Organizations aboard the* Mavi Marmara *Were Turkish and Arab Islamic Extremists Led by IHH* (26 September 2010), paras. 2, 9, 11. But in the Israeli information packet distributed just before the commando assault, IHH was benignly described as "a Turkish pro-Palestinian human rights organization with a strong Muslim orientation ... which provides humanitarian relief into areas of war and conflict." Military Strategic Information Section, International Military Cooperation Department, Strategic Division, Israel Defense Forces, "Free Gaza Flotilla" (27 May 2010).

7. *Report of the Fact-Finding Mission*, paras. 112–14. A semi-official Israeli publication did not dispute that "gas, stun, and smoke grenades were fired from the [Israeli] boats" immediately as they approached the *Mavi Marmara*, while a largely apologetic *New York Times* reconstruction conceded that "the crack of an Israeli sound grenade and a hail of rubber bullets from above were supposed to disperse activists" *before* the commandos hit the deck of the *Mavi Marmara*. Intelligence and Terrorism Information Center, *Preparations Made by IHH for Confrontation with the IDF and the Violence Exercised by That Organization's Operatives* (15 September 2010), para. 11; Sabrina Tavernise and Ethan Bronner, "Days of Planning Led to Flotilla's Hour of Chaos," *New York Times* (4 June 2010).

8. One passenger on the *Mavi Marmara* had apparently been convicted and served prison time for his involvement in the 1996 hijacking of a Russian ferryboat. (The hijackers were demanding the release of Chechen prisoners.)

9. Hugh Pope, "Erdogan is Not the Bogeyman," *Haaretz* (18 June 2010); International Crisis Group, *Turkey's Crises over Israel and Iran* (8 September 2010), p. 7; *Report of the Fact-Finding Mission*, para. 129. The passengers had to break into medical supplies earmarked for Gaza in order to treat the wounded.

10. *Report of the Fact-Finding Mission*, paras. 101, 116, 165. Israel has not produced any evidence substantiating its claim that passengers fired live ammunition at the commandos, while its public statements on this point have been riddled with inconsistencies and contradictions (ibid., p. 26n70).

11. Ibid., paras. 125–26.

12. Robert Booth, "Gaza Flotilla Activists Were Shot in Head at Close Range," *Guardian* (4 June 2010); *Report of the Fact-Finding Mission*, paras. 118, 120, 170. About 50 passengers suffered injuries. Israel reported six to ten commandos injured, two seriously.

13. Ben Knight, "Claim and Counterclaim after Deadly Flotilla Raid," *ABC News* (1 June 2010).

14. Nahum Barnea, "The Test of the Result," *Yediot Ahronot* (1 June 2010); Ben Kaspit, "It's Not Enough to Be Right," *Maariv* (1 June 2010); Amos Harel, "Straight into the Trap," *Haaretz* (1 June 2010); Mordechai Kedar, "A War for World's Future," *ynetnews.com* (31 May 2010; http://tinyurl.com/2bzf5qb); Mickey Bergman, "The IDF Soldiers Were Sent on a Mission That Defies Logic," *Huffington Post* (1 June 2010); Yaakov Katz, "Duped," *Jerusalem Post* (4 June 2010). Flotilla passengers anticipated that "if we fail to stop, they will probably knock out our propellers or rudders, then tow us somewhere for repair"

(Henning Mankell, "Flotilla Raid Diary," in Moustafa Bayoumi, ed., *Midnight on the Mavi Marmara: The attack on the Gaza freedom flotilla and how it changed the course of the Israel/Palestine conflict* (New York: 2010), p. 22).

15. Norman G. Finkelstein, *"This Time We Went Too Far": Truth and consequences of the Gaza invasion* (New York: 2010; expanded paperback edition, 2011), p. 218, quoting from the report by the Turkel Commission (more on which below).

16. The Entebbe raid was a hostage rescue operation carried out by elite Israeli commandos at Entebbe airport in Uganda on 4 July 1976. For its significance in this context, see Finkelstein, *"This Time,"* pp. 181–82.

17. Scott Wilson, "Israel Says Free Gaza Movement Poses Threat to Jewish State," *Washington Post* (1 June 2010), quoting Itamar Rabinovich, former Israeli ambassador to the US; "Eiland: Flotilla was preventable," *Jerusalem Post* (23 July 2010).

18. *Report of the Fact-Finding Mission*, paras. 76–77.

19. O9Beirut177 Date13/02/2009 05:56 Origin Embassy Beirut Classification SECRET//NOFORM (*WikiLeaks*).

20. Amos Oz, "Israeli Force, Adrift on the Sea," *New York Times* (1 June 2010).

21. John J. Mearsheimer, "Sinking Ship," *American Conservative* (1 August 2010).

22. Katz, "Duped."

23. Kaspit, "It's Not Enough"; David Horowitz, "Analysis: The flotilla fiasco," *Jerusalem Post* (1 June 2010); Harel, "Straight into the Trap"; Charles Levinson and Jay Solomon, "Israel's Isolation Deepens," *Wall Street Journal* (3 June 2010).

24. Gideon Levy, "Operation Mini Cast Lead," *Haaretz* (1 June 2010).

25. Kaspit, "It's Not Enough."

26. Uzi Mahnaimi and Gareth Jenkins, "Operation Calamity," *Sunday Times* (6 June 2010).

27. Noam Sheizaf, "Flotilla: New *Mavi Marmara* pictures raise more questions regarding IDF attack," *Promised Land* (6 June 2010; http://tinyurl.com/2aj4qrc).

28. Ken O'Keefe, "'Soldiers Thought We Would Kill Them,'" *ynetnews.com* (7 June 2010; http://tinyurl.com/25qbopw).

29. Reuven Pedatzur, "A Failure Any Way You Slice It," *Haaretz* (1 June 2010).

30. Jeffrey Goldberg, "Says One Israeli General: 'Everybody thinks we're bananas,'" *theatlantic.com* (1 June 2010).

31. University of Maryland, in conjunction with Zogby International, *2010 Arab Public Opinion Poll.* Forty-one percent responded that Israel's power "has its strengths and weaknesses."

32. In the original text, the author predicted that Israel's next target would be Lebanon but, in the event, it proved not to be the case.

33. Jonathan Ferziger and Calev Ben-David, "Gaza Situation 'Unsustainable,' Clinton Says as Ship Approaches," *Bloomberg Businessweek* (1 June 2010); United Nations Department of Public Information, "Security Council Condemns Acts Resulting in Civilian Deaths during Israeli Operation against Gaza-Bound Aid Convoy, Calls for Investigation, in Presidential Statement" (31 May 2010). See also Bernard Kouchner, Franco Frattini, and Miguel Angel Moratinos, "Averting Another Gaza," *New York Times* (10 June 2010), "EU Strongly Condemns Gaza Flotilla Attack," *EurActiv.com* (2 June 2010), and Yossi Lempkowicz, "Gaza Flotilla: EU Parliament calls for international inquiry and end to blockade," *European Jewish Press* (17 June 2010).

34. Haneen Zoabi, "Freeing Gaza; Liberating Ourselves," in Bayoumi, ed., *Midnight*, p. 71.

35. Nicolas Pelham, "Hamas Back Out of Its Box," *Middle East Report Online* (2 September 2010).

36. "John Ging: Conditions in Gaza have not changed since Israel declared it would ease the blockade," *Middle East Monitor* (11 November 2010).

37. Sally Belfrage, *Freedom Summer* (New York: 1965), p. 130.

38. Norman G. Finkelstein, *What Gandhi Says: About nonviolence, resistance and courage* (New York: 2012).

39. James Foreman, *The Making of Black Revolutionaries* (New York: 1972), pp. 311–12.

40. Charles Levinson, "Israel's Foes Embrace New Resistance Tactics," *Wall Street Journal* (2 July 2010).

41. Finkelstein, *"This Time,"* pp. 168–80.

42. *Report of the Secretary-General's Panel of Inquiry on the 31 May 2010 Flotilla Incident* (September 2011), p. 7, para. 3. Hereafter: UN Panel. For a fuller discussion of this report, see Norman G. Finkelstein, "Torpedoing the Law: How the Palmer Report justified Israel's naval blockade of Gaza," *Insight Turkey* (Fall 2011).

43. Israel Ministry of Foreign Affairs, "Israel to Participate in UN Panel on Flotilla Events" (2 August 2010).

44. It was merely "tasked with reviewing the reports of national investigations" into the assault. UN News Centre, "UN Chief Announces Panel of Inquiry into Gaza Flotilla Incident" (2 August 2010). This panel was separate and distinct from the UN fact-finding mission appointed by the Human Rights Council that was quoted earlier.

45. International Federation for Human Rights, "FIDH Deeply Concerned by the Composition of UN Panel of Inquiry into the Flotilla Events" (6 August 2010); Colombia Support Network, "A Failed Presidency? A New Beginning?" (4 August 2010; http://tinyurl.com/2abja6x).

46. Finkelstein, *"This Time,"* pp. 195–96.

47. UN Panel, pp. 39–40, para. 71; p. 45, para. 82; see also ibid., p. 43, para. 78.

48. Amnesty International, "Suffocating Gaza: The Israeli blockade's effects on Palestinians" (1 June 2010).

49. Amnesty International, "Colombian President Should Stop False Accusations against Human Rights Group" (28 November 2008).

50. UN Panel, p. 39, para. 70.

51. Originally imposed in 1991, Israel's closure policy in Gaza was incrementally tightened as time elapsed, entering its most egregious phase in 2007. See Gisha (Legal Center for Freedom of Movement), *A Guide to the Gaza Closure: In Israel's own words* (Tel Aviv: September 2011).

52. The UN Panel, citing the Israeli Turkel Report (see following endnote), concedes that Israel's blockade policies were "designed to weaken the economy" of Gaza—but then qualifies—"in order to undermine Hamas's ability to attack Israel" (p. 69, para. 153). One can only tremble at the potency of Hamas's military arsenal if Israel had allowed bonbons to enter Gaza.

53. Public Commission to Examine the Maritime Incident of 31 May 2010, *The Turkel Commission Report, Part One* (January 2011). Hereafter: Israeli Turkel Report. For detailed analysis of this report, see Finkelstein, *"This Time,"* Appendix 2.

54. Israeli Turkel Report, pp. 56–58, my emphases.

55. Ibid., pp. 66–67. It continues: "In other words, as long as the land crossings are subject to Israeli control, there is prima facie a possibility that the opening of an additional route to the Gaza Strip, such as a maritime route that is not controlled by the State of Israel, will affect the humanitarian situation in the Gaza Strip."

56. Ibid., pp. 67–68, my emphases.

57. Ibid., p. 108.

58. For a recent restatement of this consensus opinion, see "Flotillas and the Gaza Blockade," *Diakonia* (July 2011).

59. The UN Panel's legal strategy recalls the approach of the Israel High Court in the Wall case. In July 2004, the International Court of Justice (ICJ) delivered an advisory opinion that found Israel's construction of a wall inside occupied Palestinian territory illegal. When the Israel High Court subsequently heard the case, it sought to avoid a ruling that frontally contradicted the ICJ. Taking issue with the ICJ's comprehensive finding, the High Court instead proposed that the legality of the Wall should be assessed on a segment-by-segment basis. The High Court also alleged that it possessed data mitigating Israeli culpability that was unavailable to the ICJ. Likewise, the UN Panel alleged (p. 44, para. 81) that it possessed "additional material" unavailable to the UN Human Rights Council Fact-Finding Mission, which had found the Israeli blockade illegal. For a juxtaposition of the ICJ advisory opinion and Israel High Court rulings, see Norman G. Finkelstein, *Knowing Too Much: Why the American Jewish romance with Israel is coming to an end* (New York: 2012), Appendix.

60. UN Panel, p. 39, para. 70, p. 43, para. 77.

61. Ibid., p. 45, para. 82.

62. *Contraband* denotes "goods which are ultimately destined for territory under the control of the enemy and which may be susceptible for use in armed conflict" (UK Ministry of Defense, *The Manual of the Law of Armed Conflict* (Oxford: 2005), p. 350).

63. The Israeli Turkel Report was at pains to argue that the visit and search procedure did not meet the challenge Israel confronted and was replaced by a naval blockade "only" as a last resort. Still, the report alleged (p. 58)—without authoritative citation and against common sense—that "during an armed conflict, it is lawful to impose a naval blockade, without considering alternatives."

64. UN Panel, p. 40, para. 72, citing the Israeli Turkel Report, p. 33. The three named attempts occurred in, respectively, 2001

(*Santorini*), 2002 (*Karine A*), and 2003 (*Abu Hassan*). The 2002 attempt has been disputed. The Turkel Report (p. 37) also alleged a fourth attempt in 2009 (*Tali*), but the UN Panel does not cite it, and not even the Israeli Ministry of Foreign Affairs alleged that this vessel was carrying weapons (http://tinyurl.com/aqdb7h). The UN Panel also notes that, "Most recently, Israel intercepted . . . a vessel on its way from Syria to Egypt, which carried 25 tons of weapons and ammunition suspected to be destined for Gaza" (p. 40n258). Would the UN Panel also uphold the legality of an Israeli naval blockade imposed on Egypt?

65. UN Panel, pp. 40–41, para. 72, p. 42, para. 74, citing the Israeli Turkel Report, pp. 54–56. The Israeli Turkel Report (p. 58) alleged that visit and search was impracticable because of the "virtual certainty that consent for search would not be granted by the Masters of the ships bent on reaching Gaza," and "it was not certain that the consent of the flag State would actually be obtained." The report provided no basis—because none existed—for its "virtual certainty," while in fact Israel's real problem—more on which presently—was the "virtual certainty" that it would not find any weapons after such a search and consequently had to let the ships pass. In another desperate iteration, the Israeli Turkel Report alleged (p. 60) that "a key requirement is that such a right [of visit and search] cannot be arbitrarily exercised. The challenge that confronted the Israeli authorities was to obtain sufficient information regarding the cargo and/or personnel on board the vessels in order to find a ground for suspicion that the vessel is engaged in transporting contraband, enemy combatants." But the report provided no example or illustration of how such a requirement in practice proved a hindrance. Other states have exercised the right of visit and search on the basis of reasonable suspicion in wartime; why did it work elsewhere? Additionally, the Israeli

Turkel Report alleged (p. 59) that Israel could not resort to the lesser measure of declaring Gaza's coastal waters an "exclusion zone" because "there is a lack of clarity in the law as to whether such a zone provides an authority to *only* search for contraband" (my emphasis). In other words, the problem was that declaring an "exclusion zone" did not explicitly allow Israel to turn back vessels *not* carrying contraband.

66. UN Panel, p. 40, para. 72, citing the Israeli Turkel Report, pp. 53–54 (see also Turkel Report, pp. 60, 91).

67. UN Panel, p. 27, para. 46, citing the Israeli Turkel Report, pp. 53–58, 111 (see also Turkel Report, pp. 91–92).

68. UN Panel, p. 40, para. 72, p. 42, para. 77. The UN Panel also appears to allege, copying from the Israeli Turkel Report, that the recent decrease in Hamas rocket and mortar attacks on Israel has somehow been related to the naval blockade (pp. 40–41, para. 72, citing the Israeli Turkel Report, pp. 92–93). The basis for this claim is, to put it charitably, on the thin side, not least because the UN Panel adduces no evidence that weapons *ever even reached Gaza by sea.*

69. Between August and December 2008, Israel let six vessels pass into Gaza (Israeli Turkel Report, pp. 35, 59).

70. Ibid., p. 36; my emphasis.

71. UN Panel, p. 68, para. 151.

72. Ibid., p. 43, para. 78 (see also ibid., p. 41, para. 72). The UN Panel delineates the proportionality test in this context as "whether any damage to the civilian population in Gaza caused by the naval blockade was excessive when weighed against the concrete and direct military advantage brought by its imposition."

73. Ibid., p. 87, para. 33. See also International Committee of the Red Cross, *Customary International Humanitarian Law, Volume I, Rules* (Cambridge: 2005), p. 189.

74. Israeli Turkel Report, p. 66:

> The absence of a commercial port is not a decisive factor, since it is clear that it is possible to find other ways of transporting goods arriving by sea, such as by means of unloading the goods with the help of fishing boats. Moreover, the assumption that goods cannot be transported into the Gaza Strip in the absence of a commercial port inherently contradicts the main purpose of the blockade, i.e., preventing the passage of weapons to the Gaza Strip, since, according to the same logic, it would not be at all possible to transport weapons to the Gaza Strip by sea.

75. Ibid.
76. UN Panel, p. 48, para. 92.
77. Ibid., p. 49, para. 96, p. 67, para. 148, pp. 67–68, para. 149, p. 71, para. 159.
78. See Chapter 1 above.
79. UN Panel, p. 68, para. 151, p. 69, para. 154.
80. Ibid., p. 4 (viii), p. 61, para. 134, p. 68, para. 151.
81. Israeli Turkel Report, pp. 222–25.
82. UN Panel, p. 46, paras. 86–87.
83. Ibid., p. 47, para. 89.
84. The Israeli Turkel Report flatly says (p. 66): "The goal of the Flotilla was obviously not just to break the blockade, but also to bring international pressure to bear in a bid to end the land based restrictions."
85. Compounding obscenity by imbecility, the UN Panel (p. 47, para. 88, p. 48, para. 93) also condemns this clique of publicity-plotters for not sufficiently warning the other passengers of the dangers that lurked in the event that they attempted to breach the blockade. As if the other activists who joined the flotilla hadn't a clue that Israel was capable of inflicting violence.

5/ GO AHEAD, INVADE!

1. Aluf Benn, "Israel Killed Its 'Subcontractor' in Gaza," *Haaretz*, 14 November 2012.

2. Reuven Pedatzur, "Why Did Israel Kill Jabari?," *Haaretz*, 4 December 2012.

3. International Crisis Group, *Fire and Ceasefire in a New Middle East* (22 November 2012).

4. See Chapters 2 and 3 above. For the provenance of the 99 percent figure, see the Goldstone Report (*Report of the United Nations Fact-Finding Mission on the Gaza Conflict* (25 September 2009)), para. 1188.

5. Barak Ravid, "During Gaza Operation, Netanyahu and Obama Finally Learned to Work Together," *Haaretz* (26 November 2012).

6. Inbal Orpaz, "How Does the Iron Dome Work?," *Haaretz* (19 November 2012); Charles Levinson and Adam Entous, "Israel's Iron Dome Battled to Get Off the Ground," *Wall Street Journal* (26 November 2012). For more on Iron Dome, see Chapter 6 below.

7. Dan Williams, "Some Gaza Rockets Stripped of Explosives to Fly Further," *Reuters* (18 November 2012).

8. Shortly after Pillar of Defense ended, MIT missile defense expert Theodore Postol, who initially swallowed Israeli propaganda, disputed its claims about Iron Dome (Paul Koring, "Success of Israel's Iron Dome Effectiveness Questioned," *Globe and Mail* (29 November 2012).

9. Ben Dror Yemini, "Ceasefire Now," *NRG-Ma'ariv* (18 November 2012).

10. Fares Akram, Jodi Rudoren and Alan Cowell, "Hamas Leader Dares Israel to Invade Amid Gaza Airstrikes," *New York Times* (19 November 2012).

11. See Chapter 6 below.

12. In a diplomatic side note to Netanyahu, Obama vaguely promised to "help Israel address its security needs, especially

the issue of smuggling of weapons and explosives into Gaza" (Office of the Press Secretary, The White House, 21 November 2012).

13. Barak Ravid, "Behind the Scenes of Israel's Decision to Accept Gaza Truce," *Haaretz* (22 November 2012).

14. "Turkey's Erdogan Calls Israel a 'Terrorist State,'" *Reuters* (19 November 2012).

15. For the *Mavi Marmara* assault, see Chapter 4 above.

6/ ISRAEL HAS THE RIGHT TO DEFEND ITSELF

1. Benjamin S. Lambeth, *Air Operations in Israel's War against Hezbollah: Learning from Lebanon and getting it right in Gaza* (Arlington, VA: 2011), p. 97 (preplanning); Uri Blau, "IDF Sources: Conditions not yet optimal for Gaza exit," *Haaretz* (8 January 2009), and Barak Ravid, "Disinformation, Secrecy, and Lies: How the Gaza offensive came about," *Haaretz* (28 December 2008) (preplanning).

2. Jack Khoury, "Abbas: Palestinian unity government will recognize Israel, condemn terrorism," *Haaretz* (26 April 2014); Jeffrey Heller, "Netanyahu Urges World Not to Recognize Palestinian Unity Government," *Reuters* (1 June 2014); Arab Center for Research and Policy Studies, *The US Stance on the Palestinian Unity Government* (Doha: 19 June 2014).

3. An Israeli spokesperson pinned blame for the kidnappings on a Hamas cell acting independently and Hamas's leadership later confirmed the Israeli account, but a Hamas official in Turkey alleged higher-level Hamas coordination. He would not be the first Hamas blowhard, or he might have taken an initiative unbeknownst to Hamas's leadership. Amos Harel and Yaniv Kubovich, "Revealed: Behind the scenes on the hunt to find kidnapped teens," *Haaretz* (1 July 2014); Katie Zavadski, "It Turns Out Hamas May Not Have Kidnapped and Killed the 3 Israeli Teens After All," *New York* (25 July 2014); Amos Harel,

"Notes from an Interrogation: How the Shin Beth gets the low-down on terror," *Haaretz* (2 September 2014).

4. Human Rights Watch, "Serious Violations in West Bank Operations" (3 July 2014).

5. "Netanyahu to US: 'Don't ever second-guess me again,'" *ynetnews.com* (2 August 2014; http://tinyurl.com/qbv9bzw).

6. Nathan Thrall, "Hamas's Chances," *London Review of Books* (21 August 2014); Assaf Sharon, "Failure in Gaza," *New York Review of Books* (25 September 2014).

7. Here as elsewhere, *Hamas* is used as short-hand for all Palestinian armed groups in Gaza.

8. "The Full Text of the Egyptian Ceasefire Proposal," *Haaretz* (15 July 2014); Barak Ravid, "Secret Call between Netanyahu, al-Sissi Led to Abortive Cease-fire," *Haaretz* (16 July 2014).

9. "Israel and Hamas Ceasefire Begins," *BBC* (19 June 2008); "Text of Israel-Hamas Cease-fire Agreement," *Jerusalem Post* (21 November 2012).

10. Menachem Shalev, "Netanyahu Recommends Large-Scale Expulsions," *Jerusalem Post* (19 November 1989).

11. Amnesty International, *Israel/Gaza Conflict: Questions and answers* (25 July 2014); "Jeremy Bowen's Gaza Notebook: 'I saw no evidence of Hamas using Palestinians as human shields,'" *New Statesman* (25 July 2014); Kim Sengupta, "Israel-Palestine Conflict: The myth of Hamas's human shields," *Independent* (21 July 2014). This chapter doesn't address the particularities of human rights violations by either side because the relevant reports have not yet been published at the time of writing.

12. Sudarsan Raghavan, "Month-long War in Gaza Has Left a Humanitarian and Environmental Crisis," *Washington Post* (9 August 2014).

13. Amnesty International, "UN Must Impose Arms Embargo and Mandate an International Investigation as Civilian Death Toll Rises" (11 July 2014).

14. Norman G. Finkelstein, *Knowing Too Much: Why the American Jewish romance with Israel is coming to an end* (New York: 2012), pp. 123–54.

15. Human Rights Watch, "Gaza: Airstrike deaths raise concerns on ground offensive" (22 July 2014).

16. Marissa Newman, "Israeli Official Confirms US Nixed Arms Shipment," *Times of Israel* (14 August 2014).

17. Gareth Porter, "US Avoided Threat to Act on Israel's Civilian Targeting," *Inter Press Service* (12 August 2014).

18. Ramsey Cox, "Senate Passes Resolution in Support of Israel," *The Hill* (17 July 2014); Connie Bruck, "Friends of Israel," *New Yorker* (1 September 2014).

19. David Hearst, "Saudi Crocodile Tears over Gaza," *Huffington Post* (28 July 2014).

20. "Arab League Urges 'All Parties' to Back Egypt's Gaza Truce Plan," *Arab News* (15 July 2014).

21. See Chapter 5 above.

22. Robert Kozak, "Israel Faces Latin American Backlash," *Wall Street Journal* (30 July 2014).

23. Nahum Barnea, "Tumbling into Gaza, and Climbing Out Again," *ynetnews.com* (29 July 2014; http://tinyurl.com/ppcy3rd); Nidal al-Mughrabi, "Exclusive: Hamas fighters show defiance in Gaza tunnel tour," *Reuters* (19 August 2014); Gili Cohen, "Tunnel Vision on Gazan Border," *Haaretz* (17 July 2014); Mark Perry, "Why Israel's Bombardment of Gaza's Neighborhood Left US Officers 'Stunned,'" *america .aljazeera.com* (27 August 2014; http://tinyurl.com/m6z4k3y).

24. Norman G. Finkelstein, *"This Time We Went Too Far": Truth and consequences of the Gaza invasion*, revised and expanded edition (New York: 2011), pp. 76–80.

25. Amos Harel, "Using Gaza Lessons to Prepare for Next Hezbollah War," *Haaretz* (7 August 2014).

26. Amos Harel, "Gaza War Taught Israel Time to Rethink Strategies," *Haaretz* (5 August 2014).

27. Meir Amit Intelligence and Terrorism Information Center (www.terrorism-info.org.il/en/article/20714); "Operation Protective Edge Cost Israel \$4.3 Billion," *jns.org* (6 August 2014; http://tinyurl.com/oxjrc5j).

28. Finkelstein, *"This Time,"* pp. 63, 80.

29. Theodore Postol, "The Evidence That Shows Iron Dome is Not Working," *Bulletin of the Atomic Scientists* (19 July 2014).

30. "Israel Visitor Numbers Nosedive during Gaza Offensive," *Agence France-Presse* (11 August 2014).

31. "In CNN Interview, Combative Bloomberg Says US Flight Ban a Mistake," *cnn.com* (22 July 2014; http://tinyurl.com/pl8etlk).

32. Emanual Yelin, "Were Gaza Tunnels Built to Harm Israeli Civilians?," *+972* (11 August 2014; http://tinyurl.com/ovxr9v).

33. Pierre Krähenbühl, "In the Eye of a Man-Made Storm," *Foreign Policy* (26 September 2014); Human Rights Watch, *In-Depth Look at Gaza School Attacks* (New York: 11 September 2014).

34. "Gaza: Ban condemns latest deadly attack near UN school as 'moral outrage and criminal act,'" *UN News Centre* (3 August 2014).

35. Donna Chiacu, "US Slams 'Disgraceful Shelling' of UN School in Gaza," *Haaretz* (3 August 2014).

36. Amos Harel, "Operation Protective Edge Advances with No Exit Strategy," *Haaretz* (20 July 2014), Amos Harel, "As Bulldozers Destroy Hamas' Underground Network, IDF Sees Light at End of Tunnel," *Haaretz* (1 August 2014), Amos Harel, "IDF Wary of New Gaza Ground Op Even as Diplomacy Lags," *Haaretz* (25 August 2014).

37. Gili Cohen, "Senior Officer: Hamas still able to carry out tunnel attacks against Israel," *Haaretz* (31 July 2014).

38. International law is either neutral on or supports (scholars differ) the right of a people struggling for self-determination to use force. James Crawford, *The Creation of States in International Law*, second edition (Oxford: 2006), pp. 135–37, 147; Heather A. Wilson, *International Law and the Use of Force by National Liberation Movements* (Oxford: 1988), pp. 135–36; A. Rigo Sureda, *The Evolution of the Right to Self-Determination: A study of United Nations practice* (Leiden: 1973), pp. 331, 343–44, 354.

39. http://www.icj-cij.org/docket/files/131/1671.pdf.

40. Yoram Dinstein, *The Conduct of Hostilities under the Law of International Armed Conflict* (Cambridge: 2004), pp. 35, 94.

41. See Norman G. Finkelstein and Mouin Rabbani, *How to Solve the Israel-Palestine Conflict* (forthcoming 2015).

42. Human Rights Watch, "Indiscriminate Palestinian Rocket Attacks" (9 July 2014).

43. Jean-Marie Henckaerts and Louise Doswald-Beck, *Customary International Humanitarian Law, Volume 1: Rules* (Cambridge: 2005), p. 523; A. P. V. Rogers, *Law on the Battlefield*, second edition (Manchester: 2004), p. 235.

44. *Legality of the Threat or Use of Nuclear Weapons* (8 July 1996)—Letter dated 16 June 1995 from the Legal Adviser to the Foreign and Commonwealth Office of the United Kingdom of Great Britain and Northern Ireland, together with Written Comments of the United Kingdom; Letter dated 20 June 1995 from the Acting Legal Adviser to the Department of State, together with Written Statement of the Government of the United States of America; Oral Statement of US representative (15 November 1995); Dissenting Opinion of Vice-President Schwebel. The ICJ itself elected not to rule on the legality of belligerent reprisals, para. 46.

45. Amira Hass, "Hamas's Rejection of the Cease-fire Deal Was a Foregone Conclusion," *Haaretz* (16 July 2014).

CONCLUSION

1. Alessandria Masi, "Israeli Airstrikes on Gaza Collapse Apartment Building," *International Business Times* (23 August 2014).

2. These figures are rounded off.

3. Nidal al-Mughrabi and Luke Baker, "What's in the Gaza Peace Deal?," *Reuters* (26 August 2014).

4. Barak Ravid, "Netanyahu: Gaza op was great military, political achievement," *Haaretz* (28 August 2014).

5. Zvi Bar'el, "With Truce, Israel Talks to Hamas and Islamic Jihad," *Haaretz* (27 August 2014).

6. Barak Ravid, "Netanyahu Saw His Chance to Run Away from Gaza, and He Took It," *Haaretz* (26 August 2014).

7. Mouin Rabbani, "Israel's 'Operation Status Quo,'" *Norwegian Peace-building Resource Center* (25 August 2014).

8. Jassem Al Salami, "Rockets and Iron Dome, the Case of Lebanon," *Offiziere.ch* (5 August 2014; offiziere.ch/?p=17519); "Israel Preparing for 'Very Violent' War against Hezbollah, TV Report Says," *Times of Israel* (6 September 2014).

9. Yossi Verter, "Netanyahu after the War: Less popular, but still unchallenged," *Haaretz* (29 August 2014).

10. Khaled Abu Toameh, "Ismail Haniyeh Makes First Appearance since Start of Gaza Operation," *Jerusalem Post* (27 August 2014).

11. Jack Khoury, "Meshal: Hamas will go back to war against Israel if upcoming truce talks fail," *Haaretz* (28 August 2014); Amira Hass, "Hamas Trying to Sell 'Victory' to Gazans," *Haaretz* (27 August 2014).

12. "Gaza Blockade—No Signs of Loosening," *IRIN* (2 September 2014).

13. "Netanyahu: Regional changes promise new 'diplomatic horizon,'" *Haaretz* (20 August 2014).

14. Norman G. Finkelstein and Mouin Rabbani, *How to Solve the Israel-Palestine Conflict* (forthcoming 2015).

15. "Hamas Popularity 'Surges after Gaza War,'" *aljazeera.com* (2 September 2014; http://tinyurl.com/k48jpyt).

16. David Rothkopf, "The US-Israeli Relationship Arrives at a Moment of Reckoning," *Foreign Policy* (26 August 2014).

17. "UN Rights Council Appoints Members of Commission to Investigate Purported Gaza Violations," *UN News Centre* (11 August 2014).

18. Tovah Lazaroff, "UNHRC Investigator Schabas Stays Mum on Hamas as 'Terror Group,'" *Jerusalem Post* (12 August 2014).

19. Norman G. Finkelstein, *"This Time We Went Too Far": Truth and consequences of the Gaza invasion*, revised and expanded edition (New York: 2011), pp. 142–43, 194–95.

20. Julian Borger, "Hague Court under Western Pressure Not to Open Gaza War Crimes Inquiry," *Guardian* (17 August 2014).

21. Fatou Bensouda, "The Truth about the ICC and Gaza," *Guardian* (29 August 2014); Yonah Jeremy Bob, "ICC: Palestine is a state, can file war crimes complaints against Israel, if chooses," *Jerusalem Post* (31 August 2014).

22. Anshel Pfeffer, "Israel Has Little to Fear from the International Criminal Court," *Haaretz* (20 May 2014).

23. Norman G. Finkelstein, *Beyond Chutzpah: On the misuse of anti-Semitism and the abuse of history*, expanded paperback edition (Berkeley: 2008), pp. 156–58 (torture), 214–16 (hostage taking).

24. Khaled Abu Toameh, "PA to Tell UN: Force Israel out of W. Bank, or we'll seek war crimes charges in The Hague," *Jerusalem Post* (28 August 2014).

25. Taylor Branch, *Parting the Waters: America in the King years, 1954–1963* (New York: 1988), pp. 756–802.

KNOWING TOO MUCH

Why the American Jewish Romance with Israel is Coming to an End

Norman G. Finkelstein

ISBN 978-1-935928-77-5 paperback
ISBN 978-1-935928-78-2 e-book
492 pages

"Finkelstein makes this argument crisply and convincingly. . . . [His] research is certainly thorough. His characterisations, too, can be brilliant, and he spares nobody."

—THE ECONOMIST

WHAT GANDHI SAYS
About Nonviolence, Resistance and Courage

Norman G. Finkelstein

ISBN 978-1-935928-79-9 paperback
ISBN 978-1-935928-80-5 e-book
100 pages

"Many of us believe we know who Gandhi was and what he represented. The truth is something quite different, and important. As Norman said to me when he gave me this tiny volume, you can read it in one sitting. That will be an essential sitting for anyone who is interested in the matter of genuine courage in the pursuit of just goals."

—JULIAN ASSANGE

"THIS TIME WE WENT TOO FAR"
Truth and Consequences of the Gaza Invasion

Norman G. Finkelstein

ISBN 978-1-935928-43-0 paperback
ISBN 978-1-935928-44-7 e-book
343 pages

"Exceptional and courageous scholarship.... Despite the changing and widening discourse on the Israeli-Palestinian conflict in the United States that now allows for greater dissent and legitimizes criticism of Israeli policy—something this book also examines in considerable detail—the struggle remains acute. This work, among Finkelstein's many others, remains an essential and critical part of that struggle."

—SARA ROY, *JOURNAL OF PALESTINE STUDIES*

OLD WINE, BROKEN BOTTLE
Ari Shavit's Promised Land

Norman G. Finkelstein

ISBN 978-1-939293-46-6 paperback
ISBN 978-1-939293-47-3 e-book
100 pages

"Where pundits perceive insight and depth, *Old Wine, Broken Bottle* points out a naked emperor spouting torrents of high-flown, perfectly meaningless rhetoric.... [A] highly effective shredding of scholarly pretension and a well-merited character assassination."

—TIM HOLMES, *NEW LEFT PROJECT*

NORMAN G. FINKELSTEIN is an activist and a scholar, and the author of a number of books, among them: *Old Wine, Broken Bottle: Ari Shavit's Promised Land*; *Knowing Too Much: Why the American Jewish Romance with Israel is Coming to an End*; *What Gandhi Says: About Nonviolence, Resistance and Courage*; *"This Time We Went Too Far": Truth and Consequences of the Gaza Invasion*; *Beyond Chutzpah: On the Misuse of Anti-Semitism and the Abuse of History* and *The Holocaust Industry: Reflections on the Exploitation of Jewish Suffering.*